COMPANY LAW

100
Questions and Answers

Company Law

Prepared by

CHART FOULKS LYNCH

HOLT, RINEHART AND WINSTON
LONDON · NEW YORK · SYDNEY · TORONTO

Holt, Rinehart and Winston Ltd: 1 St Anne's Road,
Eastbourne, East Sussex BN21 3UN

British Library Cataloguing in Publication Data

Chart Foulks Lynch
100 questions and answers on company law.
1. Corporation law—England—Problems, exercises, etc.
I. Title
344.206′66′076 KD2079

ISBN 0–03–910436–2

Printed in Great Britain by Spottiswoode Ballantyne Ltd., Colchester and London

Last digit is print number: 9 8 7 6 5 4 3 2 1

ACKNOWLEDGEMENTS

We wish to thank the following bodies for permission to use questions from their examination papers:

Institute of Chartered Accountants in England and Wales
Association of Certified Accountants
Institute of Cost and Management Accountants

INTRODUCTION

A book full of questions and answers could be the single most important purchase that you as a student make in preparing for your examination.

Having experienced similar questions before sitting down to the real thing will give you a tremendous advantage. Having actually answered, say, fifty questions on the same topics as those to be examined must give you a good chance of meeting the ambiguities, peculiarities of terminology and downright catches that crop up in any paper.

In this book we have drawn questions from the main accounting bodies but we have not individually identified them as to source or date. The reasons we hope are obvious. Almost all the questions could have been posed by any of the accounting bodies concerned—standards are very similar and style and emphasis vary only slightly. Also, due to changing legislation we have adapted many questions to cater for the *Finance Act 1982* and *Companies Act 1981*, for instance, and it would not be fair to attribute credit or blame in these circumstances.

Dates can be misleading as students try to discern trends. These trends can best be identified from the students' own magazines, newsletters and journals. The questions we have selected generally will be examined, albeit in some disguise, on many future occasions.

The book itself is divided into main subject areas to help you select relevant questions. If you have time, treat it as a workbook—if not, use it as a final topping-up exercise.

We hope it helps to bring you examination success.

EXAMINATION TECHNIQUE

Sensible preparation and excellent examination technique will help you succeed in (if not enjoy) your forthcoming examinations.

Contained in the following few pages are some guidelines to smooth your path through the fast approaching ordeal.

Part 1—The Build-up

This vital time must concentrate on full and structured revision. There is no escape from hard work, but for optimum benefit there are some rules:

Plan your revision time

(a) Write down your revision plan, giving yourself plenty of time to revise each subject in full.
(b) Don't concentrate so much on your weak subjects that you ignore your strong ones.
(c) Do lots of questions against the clock to build up your speed. A very large proportion of candidates who fail an exam do so because they run out of time, not because they lack the basic knowledge.

Plan your leisure also

(a) Work done after midnight or when you are tired is counterproductive. You will not be able to concentrate and you will make mistakes.
(b) If you have time off work to study, try to keep to roughly similar office hours plus say 7.00–9.00 in the evening. Work Saturdays but have a break on Sunday.

Stick to your plan

(a) Despite your plan there is a great temptation to spend too much time on one subject. Don't.
(b) Beware the dreaded tipsters. Tipsters don't know, they can only guess, and with a wide syllabus, concentrating on one or two topics is very dangerous.

The day before

(a) Relax as much as possible. If you haven't done enough work by now you won't have enough time to make up the difference. The only work you *must* do is ensuring you know where and when you are taking the exams and checking train and bus timetables to ensure you get there in good time.

(b) Do what you like doing—play the harp, torment the cat, pore over your stamp collection. If your hobby is drinking, *don't!*
(c) Overhaul your equipment. New calculator batteries and some spares, plenty of sharp pencils and full pens, are all essential.
(d) Go to bed early.

The aim is to rest so that you are on top form next morning. You will appreciate this when you turn up at the examination hall and encounter in the foyer the haggard faced and bleary eyed who are frantically borrowing pencil sharpeners. If they are tired before they start, think what they will feel like after the first two papers.

Part 2—In the Examination Room

This is the point at which you undergo a metamorphosis into a ruthless 'mark grubber'. Any examiner's report invariably will refer to at least half of the points listed below, and students, when reading of such basic errors, vow that they would never have been so stupid. This vow generally lasts until the moment they enter the examination room!

Attend to detail

'Topping and tailing' should be practised on all possible occasions. Underlining headings, using £ signs, dates and so on, all help to pick up any presentation and discretion marks available.

Don't annoy the examiner

Submit your questions in the right order. Don't use words like 'obviously' and 'of course' too often. Don't be critical of any specific question or the paper in general.

Examiners are only human (we think) and such behaviour is bound to upset them. You cannot afford to waste even half a mark when your career is at stake, so play the game by their rules and change the system afterwards if you feel strongly about it.

Workings

Refer specifically to workings and put them in order, clearly labelled. Don't allow the examiner merely to stumble on them by accident.

Remember, random jottings around a page will not attract as many marks as a carefully sequenced set of workings, even if the same information is present. You will be expected to order your thoughts and present information/reports when qualified, so the examiners have a right to expect similar treatment now.

Answer the question

There are many faults under this heading:

(i) Overkill—seeing a particular word in the question and writing all there is to know about that subject. It may have nothing much to do with the real question you have been asked.

(ii) Woods and trees—being unable to identify the major mark-carrying areas, or possibly devoting fifteen minutes to part (c) of a question carrying only 3 marks while writing only a few lines on part (a) carrying, say, 12 marks.

(iii) Not reading the question. A question may ask for a report or a letter, but some students nevertheless steadfastly produce essays or lists or anything but the required format.

(iv) Rewriting the question! Many students believe (mistakenly) that they can, in effect, alter the emphasis of a question, or even change it completely. Only answer the specific question set.

What I meant to say was . . .

You cannot stand at the examiner's shoulder and explain the real meaning of your script or terminology. Say what you mean and leave nothing to chance. Communication is a two way process. You have first to absorb and understand what is being asked. But having got the message you must then formulate your answer in as understandable a way as possible. Both parts are equally fundamental.

Arrange your answer in a logical sequence

Spending a few moments jotting down the main points of your answer and assembling them in a logical order will pay handsome dividends. After all, jottings on a narrative question are the equivalent of ordinary figure workings for a computational problem.

Treat the examiner as an intelligent layman

You must not assume the examiner knows certain things. He probably does, but you haven't proved to him that you do if you leave such matters out altogether.

You will probably feel less self-conscious in explaining carefully the way in which a bad debts account works if you assume that the examiner is an intelligent layman.

But, remember also that, since the examiner is most definitely not a layman, he will not tolerate wrong statements. Don't bluff!

Use of abbreviations

Using abbreviations like confetti can cause problems, particularly where non-standard abbreviations are thrown in for good measure. CCA, I/REV,

MCT, SSAP are acceptable (but not many people know that G.I.N. means goods inwards note).

If you do use initials, always put the full meaning in on the first occasion (followed by its abbreviation).

Check whether answer is reasonable

Whenever you produce an answer to a computational question spend a few seconds asking yourself whether the solution arrived at is sensible. It is so easy to press the wrong calculator button and you must give yourself every chance of picking up these silly errors.

Answer all questions

You have 180 minutes to try for 100 marks and therefore can allocate 1.8 minutes for each mark on the paper.

Don't overrun your time on each question as you are far more likely to pick up the first five marks of a new question than the last five marks of an earlier one.

1. Don't panic—two or three deep breaths as soon as you sit down will help calm you.

   Try to ensure you are not caught out by some unexpected event. To this end find out what types of examination paper are used and check which rates and allowances you are to be provided with.
2. You are only trying to pass the paper, not (necessarily) achieve 100%. There *will* be things you don't know so don't leave the examination room after the first exam in a black depression simply because you failed to deal fully with parts 3(a) and 4(c) of a paper.
3. Remember the three R's. Perhaps the best piece of advice we can give is to obey the three R's *in the following order*:

   Read
   Reflect
   Write!

   Good luck with your examinations.

CONTENTS

?

Questions

QUESTION A1

Smith contracted to sell his house to Jones but later changed his mind and no longer wished to complete the sale. He was afraid that Jones might obtain from the court an order for specific performance of the contract of sale. Smith therefore transferred the house to a company of which he was the sole owner in exchange for shares. Jones wants the house; he is not interested in claiming damages since he has not suffered any loss.

Advise him.

QUESTION A2

Susan, Mabel and Doris wish to carry on business as caterers. They all intend to take part in the management of the business but would like to avoid personal liability for its debts. They are anxious that the affairs of the business and the arrangements between themselves should be kept secret as far as possible, and would like to be able to transfer their respective interests in the business without difficulty.

Disregarding tax considerations, advise them whether it would be better for them to form a company limited by shares or a partnership and state the advantages and disadvantages of each.

QUESTION A3

The objects clause of X Ltd states as one of its objects the carrying on of the business of managing cinemas; it has been carrying on such a business for many years. The directors now wish to undertake the management of a chain of restaurants and at the same time to change the name of the company to Good Food Ltd. In this scheme they have the support of shareholders who (with the directors themselves) own 82% of the company's issued shares. Some at least of the other shareholders are opposed to the scheme.

Advise the directors whether and if so how these changes may be made.

QUESTION A4

X Ltd incorporated in 1980 has articles of association which provide that Patrick shall be managing director for life. Y Ltd, which has acquired 90% of the shares of X Ltd, intends to cancel this article and to remove Patrick from the board of directors altogether.

(*a*) *Can Patrick prevent this alteration of the articles?*
(*b*) *If he is dismissed from his post of managing director can he recover damages?* (Ignore statutory rules on notice and unfair dismissal.)

QUESTION A5

Developer believes that the hotels of an old-established hotel company could be more profitably employed by being converted into offices, and is endeavouring to gain control of the company. The board of directors proposes to sell the hotels and apply one half of the proceeds towards paying the company's employees' and directors' redundancy compensation payments in excess of those prescribed by law and their contracts with the company.

Advise a minority shareholder who supports Developer.

QUESTION A6

Charles has a minority shareholding in a family company; he is on bad terms with his cousins, who are the directors. Charles recently tried to transfer part of his shareholding to his son but the directors refused to register the transfer and ignored his request to give reasons for their decision. Charles has now decided to invoke a clause in the articles of association by which if a member wishes to transfer his shares the directors must if he so requests purchase the shares equally between them at a fair value. The directors have refused to purchase the shares.

Advise Charles whether the directors are justified in their acts of refusal.

QUESTION A7

James owns 90% of the issued share capital of a private limited company and his two sons own the remaining 10%. It irks James that the company's accounts are required to be filed at the Companies Registry and are therefore open to public inspection.

Advise James whether it is possible for the company to avoid making its accounts available for public inspection and if so, what procedure must be followed and whether any other consequences will ensue.

QUESTION A8

Railtrack Plc is incorporated with the sole object of manufacturing and laying railway track in England. It had been hoped to secure a contract in connection with railways to be constructed on the approach routes to a Channel Tunnel but the prospect of securing such contracts now seems remote. The directors have decided that there are only two ways in which their expertise can be profitably employed. The first is to contract for the renovation and modernisation of railways in the USA, where the energy crisis has resulted in plans for a return to railway transport. The other is to sub-contract for equipment to be used on new cross-channel ferry boats.

Advise the directors.

QUESTION A9

A and B are forming a company whose main object will be to acquire from C his wholesale manufacturing business. The company cannot be formed until certain legal points have been cleared up. C is becoming impatient and insists that A and B shall enter into a contract with C immediately for the purchase of the business by the company.

Advise A and B.

QUESTION A10

In what circumstances, if any, may shareholders manage their company?

QUESTION A11

Exe Plc has articles of association in the form of *Table A* (*Companies Act 1948*). No managing director has ever been appointed and the day-to-day business of the company has been conducted by John, the chairman. The board of directors is aware of the position and has never raised any objection.

Advise Norman, who has entered into contracts with the company through John. (It now appears that these contracts are not authorised by the objects clause in the memorandum of association of Exe Plc.)

QUESTION A12

The articles of association of Aire Ltd provide that Donald and Charles are to be employed as sales manager and accountant respectively at salaries of not less than £10,000 per annum until they attain the age of 65 years. They have both been so employed for many years and are now in their late fifties.

(*a*) *Advise Donald, who has received notice from the company purporting to discharge him. He does not wish to leave.*
(*b*) *Advise Charles, who has offered his resignation which has been rejected by the company.*

QUESTION A13

Don Plc has as its main object the business of travel agents, but there are subsidiary objects, including one which authorises the company 'to borrow money' and another which permits the company 'to carry on any business which the directors consider to be profitable'. The travel agency has closed and the directors have now approached Money Bank for a loan to build a factory for the manufacture of shoes.

Discuss.

QUESTION A14

Wharfe & Partners is an old established family business. Terry has agreed with the partners to incorporate a private company to acquire this business and the partners have agreed to sell to the company. Terry has filed the necessary papers for registration but the certificate of incorporation has not yet been issued. The partners now consider that the business is worth far more than the sale price and they wish to avoid the agreement.

Discuss.

QUESTION A15

In Salomon's Case (1897), which arguments were successful in the earlier stages and overruled by the House of Lords?

QUESTION A16

Smith and Brown have arranged to form a company to take over and run a business to be purchased from Jones. Evans is to subscribe the greater part of the share capital but Smith and Brown will be the first directors. The papers for the formation of the company were presented at the Companies Registry early in December with a request that the certificate of incorporation might be issued on 1 Jan. However, the Registrar returned the papers after the Christmas holiday pointing out that although they were otherwise in order the signatures of the subscribers to the memorandum of association had not been witnessed. That omission was remedied and the papers re-presented to the Registry on 31 Dec. The Registrar said that he would not now be able to issue his certificate of incorporation until 7 Jan. Arrangements which cannot now be altered had been made to hold a meeting on 2 Jan. at which Smith and Brown would sign the contract on behalf of the company for the purchase of the business at a price of £20,000 and £25,000 ordinary shares of £1 each would be allotted for cash to Smith, Brown and Evans.

Smith and Brown have decided to hold the meeting as arranged on 2 Jan. believing that the matter will be regularised when the certificate of incorporation is issued a few days later.

Advise them.

QUESTION A17

A, B and C have joined forces to manufacture and market a new electronic device. For this purpose they have bought a company 'off the shelf' from a firm specialising in company formation. The authorised share capital is £10,000 in £1 shares of which A and B have subscribed for 1,000 shares each and C for 500. A, B and C are the only directors. The objects clause defines the main object as carrying on the business of general merchants; the articles are substantially in the form of *Table A*. More capital is needed; A and B have found X, a financier who is willing to subscribe for 1,000 shares and to provide a substantial loan but insists that (i) the company must have a more appropriate main object and (ii) the articles must be altered to provide that any member holding 1,000 shares may appoint one director. C does not like X and is opposed to admitting him to the company on these terms.

Can C successfully oppose the scheme and if so how?

QUESTION A18

What is 'the veil of incorporation'? Give four examples of circumstances in which exceptions are made and the veil is lifted.

QUESTION A19

Harry sent a letter on the printed letterhead of X Ltd accepting an offer by Tom to supply goods to X Ltd. Harry signed himself 'Director, for and on behalf of X Ltd'. Tom, who had previously supplied and been paid for goods ordered by Harry in this way, duly sent the goods in compliance with the latest order. X Ltd has gone into liquidation and the liquidator refuses to pay for the last consignment ordered by Harry on the grounds that (i) the goods were required for an *ultra vires* purpose and (ii) Harry had not been authorised by X Ltd to order the goods. Tom has now inspected the memorandum and articles of association of X Ltd for the first time and finds that on the *ultra vires* point the liquidator may be right; the articles are substantially in the form of *Table A*.

Advise Tom.

QUESTION A20

'. . . the fundamental attribute of corporate personality . . . is that the Corporation is a legal entity distinct from its members'.

State which in your opinion are the two outstanding advantages of incorporation and explain their dependence upon this fundamental attribute.

QUESTION A21

(*a*) *Why does a company have a registered office, how may the situation of the registered office be changed and what limit is placed on such variation?*
(*b*) *What are the statutory requirements regarding the particulars to be disclosed on company letters and bills?*

QUESTION A22

(*a*) *What are the legal characteristics of a new public company limited by shares?*
(*b*) *Give three ways in which a new public company differs from a private company.*
(*c*) *What steps must be taken in order to convert a private company into a new public company?*

QUESTION A23

The objects clause of the memorandum of Road Haulage Ltd contains the following main objects:

(a) to buy and operate all types of mechanically propelled vehicles;
(b) to buy land and erect buildings for the purposes of the company's business;
(c) to do all such things as are incidental to the above objects.

The business of the company is at present that of haulage contractor but the directors wish to widen the scope of the business so as to operate taxicabs and also to use the premises of the company as a retail motor garage and to buy, sell and repair cars. A minority group of members is opposed to the directors' proposals.

Advise the directors.

QUESTION A24

John and James are the subscribers to the memorandum of association of Zed Ltd, a company limited by shares, which is in the process of formation. The documents are now ready to be filed with the Registrar of Companies.

One of the objects of Zed Ltd is to purchase the business of Zed and Co from Tom Zed, the surviving partner, who wishes to retire. Tom Zed is insisting that a contract for the sale of the firm's undertaking to the company shall be signed forthwith.

Advise John and James.

QUESTION A25

The articles of association of Lees Ltd authorise the board to appoint a managing director and to revoke the appointment when they think fit. The board appointed Jim managing director 'for so long as he shall remain a director of the company.' Jim is still a director but the board has resolved to revoke his appointment as managing director forthwith.

Advise Jim.

QUESTION A26

Consider and give reasons for the changes made by the Companies Act 1980 in relation to the designation and classification of public and private limited companies.

QUESTION A27

You are approached by Jerry and Tom who carry on the business of building contractors under the name 'Jerry Builders'. In view of a recession in the building trade they wish to obtain the benefits of limited liability. They instruct you to incorporate their business, which is presently worth £30,000 and which is owned equally by Jerry and Tom.

Describe the steps which would be necessary in order to carry out these instructions.

QUESTION A28

(a) The *Companies Act 1948* provides that 'On the registration of the memorandum of a company the registrar shall certify under his hand that the company is *incorporated* and, in the case of a *limited* company, that the company is *limited*.'

Discuss the meaning of the terms 'incorporated' and 'limited' in this context.

(b) 'In exceptional cases, the law either goes behind the corporate personality to the individual members, or ignores the separate personality of each company in favour of the economic reality constituted by a group of associated concerns' (L. C. B. Gower—*Principles of Modern Company Law*).

Give one example under the Companies Acts, and one under the general law, of the exceptional circumstances in which the court will go behind or ignore the corporate personality.

QUESTION A29

(*a*) *What legal effect is given to a contract purporting to be made on behalf of a company which had not been formed at the time of contracting?*
(*b*) *Can a company, upon incorporation, ratify such a contract?*
(*c*) *What are the rules governing the power of a company incorporated under the Companies Acts to ratify a contract, made on its behalf, which is clearly beyond the objects of the company as defined in the memorandum?*

QUESTION A30

(*a*) *By what procedure and for what purposes may a company alter its objects?*
(*b*) *How may such a proposal be challenged?*
(*c*) *What is the value of a power to alter the objects since the enactment of the European Communities Act 1972?*

QUESTION A31

The *Companies Act 1948, s. 20* provides that '...the memorandum and articles shall, when registered, bind the company and the members thereof to the same extent as if they respectively had been signed and sealed by each member, and contained covenants on the part of each member to observe all the provisions of the memorandum and of the articles'.

Explain, with ONE example for each from decided cases, the effect of this section of the Act on:

(*a*) *a member who wishes to enforce his rights under the articles against his company;*
(*b*) *a member who wishes to enforce his rights under the articles against other members;*
(*c*) *rights given by or under the articles to a person other than in his capacity as a member.*

QUESTION B1

The ordinary £1 shares of X Plc are being dealt with on the open market at £3 each. The directors propose to raise £500,000 of additional capital by issuing 200,000 existing unissued shares of £1 at a price of £2.50 per share.

What legal rules should they be advised they must observe?

QUESTION B2

Anthony was recently allotted shares by Red Plc on the basis of a fraudulent prospectus.

Advise Anthony:

(*a*) *whether he should or should not attend the next Annual General Meeting and protest about the misstatements in the prospectus;*
(*b*) *whether he should vote for or against the payment of any dividend proposed at that meeting;*
(*c*) *whether he should sell the shares, and if so, if he should sell them now or wait until they go 'ex-div';*
(*d*) *whether there is any other action open to him before the Annual General Meeting.*

QUESTION B3

(*a*) *What is the effect of the certification of any instrument of transfer by a company of shares in that company and when is such certification necessary?*
(*b*) *If a company secretary makes a mistake in the certification of a transfer what is the extent of the company's liability?*

QUESTION B4

Alex agrees to pay £750,000 for a controlling interest in Shops Plc if the company will transfer the £1m deposited with its present bankers to the merchant bankers from which Alex has arranged to borrow £750,000 as a guarantee for Alex's loan. After the transfer the merchant bank honours a cheque drawn by Alex to pay for 51% of the equity of Shops Plc.

Discuss.

QUESTION B5

The *Companies Act 1948* provides that a condition in any debenture shall not be invalid by reason only that the debentures are thereby made irredeemable or redeemable only on the happening of a contingency, however remote, or on the expiration of a period, however long, any rule of equity to the contrary notwithstanding.

Explain:

(*a*) *what rule of equity is involved;*
(*b*) *the significance of the inclusion of the words 'by reason only';*
(*c*) *whether, if the debentures are expressed to be irredeemable, this means that the lender has parted with his money for all time.*

QUESTION B6

Smith has just been appointed receiver of the undertaking and assets of a small manufacturing company under a floating charge, created six months ago to secure additional loan facilities provided by the company's bank. Smith finds that the main cause of the company's serious financial position is that some time ago, when demand for its products was slack, it accepted orders at very low prices. These contracts have not yet been completed by delivery of the products but Smith can see that they are likely to be barely profitable. The market is now more active; if the company's output for the next few months was not already committed to the existing contracts Smith could obtain orders for immediate delivery at much higher prices. But the new orders would be subject to stringent conditions as to the quality of the products to be supplied, about which Smith has his doubts.

What legal principles should he bear in mind in deciding these questions of commercial strategy?

QUESTION B7

Blue Ltd, haulage contractors, in Jan. 1981 issued a debenture in favour of Money Bank Ltd. This debenture contains a fixed charge of the premises of the company and a floating charge of its assets and undertaking. In Aug. 1981 the bank appointed a receiver and manager of the company. The receiver in the course of his preliminary investigation noticed that the debenture had not been entered in the company's own register of charges.

What are the legal implications of these facts?

QUESTION B8

On 1 Jan. Y Ltd created a floating charge over its assets in favour of A as security for a loan of £20,000 which was duly made by A; the charge was not registered under *s. 95 CA 1948*. On 1 Feb. Y Ltd created a second floating charge in favour of B Bank as security for an existing overdraft of

£50,000; the charge prohibited Y Ltd from creating charges of any kind which would rank in priority to B's charge; B's charge was duly registered. On 1 Mar. Y Ltd purchased a freehold factory from C at a price of £100,000 and made a part payment of £20,000; a fixed charge over the factory to secure the balance of £80,000 outstanding was created in favour of C and was duly registered.

(*a*) A has now discovered that his charge was not registered as it should have been. *Can he remedy the position and if so how and to what extent?*
(*b*) B has now discovered the existence of C's charge. *Can B claim priority over C?*

QUESTION B9

The authorised share capital of Traders Ltd is £15,000 divided into 12,000 ordinary and 3,000 preference shares all of £1 each; all the shares have been issued and are fully paid. The preference shareholders are entitled to a non-cumulative preference dividend of 6% pa on the amount paid up on their shares; in all other respects they have the same rights as ordinary shareholders. Class rights may (under the articles of association) be varied with the consent of the holders of three quarters of the shares of the class.

Traders has suffered heavy losses; the directors propose to cancel the issued share capital of both classes to the extent of 80p per share, thus producing ordinary and preference shares of 20p instead of £1.

(*a*) *What is the procedure for effecting these changes?*
(*b*) *Have the preference shareholders any good reason for objecting to the scheme?*
(*c*) *If so are they in a position to prevent it being effected?*

QUESTION B10

Ernest has been appointed receiver and manager of Exe Ltd as a result of a debenture holders' action. The company is not in liquidation.

(*a*) *Is Ernest liable personally for contracts which he makes in the course of carrying out his duties?*
(*b*) *Must he fulfil contracts entered into by the company prior to his appointment?*
(*c*) *What is the effect of the appointment on the position of the directors of the company?*

QUESTION B11

The directors of A Ltd, which was incorporated last month, propose to issue £1 shares of the company in exchange for 50p shares of B Ltd on the basis of a straight 1 for 1 exchange of shares.

State the relevant legal rules if the net asset values of the shares of B Ltd at the time of the exchange is:

(a) £1.25p per share and (b) 75p per share.

None of the existing members of A Ltd wish to purchase additional shares. *Would your answer differ if A were a public limited company?*

QUESTION B12

In the context of prospectus law what is:

(a) an offer for sale,
(b) a statement of adjustments,
(c) an underwriting commission.

State in each case how information of the terms is made available to the public.

QUESTION B13

Distinguish the purpose of appointing a trustee for debenture holders from that of appointing a receiver and manager for debenture holders. Indicate when each would be appointed and by whom the appointment would be made.

QUESTION B14

The authorised issue and fully paid share capital of Z Ltd is £10,000 divided into 4,500 6% preference shares of £1 each, all held by Smith, and 5,500 ordinary shares of £1 each, all held by Jones. Under the articles of association, which follow the model of *Table A*, (1) each share of every class carries one vote, (2) a subdivision of shares may be effected by passing an ordinary resolution, and (3) dividend entitlement is in proportion to the amount paid up on each share. Jones proposes at the next general meeting to pass a resolution to subdivide his £1 ordinary shares into 22,000 ordinary shares of 25p each. Smith considers that such a change would be prejudicial to him and that it amounts to a variation of his rights as holder of the preference shares.

How would it be prejudicial to Smith and can he prevent it?

QUESTION B15

The issued share capital of Ash, a limited company, consists of fully paid ordinary shares of £1 each. The board of directors have decided that it would be appropriate to repay to shareholders 75p per share, leaving the shares as shares of 25p each, fully paid.

Indicate the procedure necessary to fulfil the legal requirements which would have to be observed to give effect to the proposal.

QUESTION B16

A Ltd has agreed to lend £10,000 to B Ltd on the security of a floating charge to be created by B Ltd over its assets and undertaking.

(*a*) *What considerations must be borne in mind and what steps taken to ensure that the charge will be valid and enforceable?*
(*b*) *In what circumstances will the charge become enforceable?*

QUESTION B17

In what circumstances (if any) and on what conditions may a company limited by shares do each of the following:

(*a*) *be the registered holder of its own shares acquired by purchase;*
(*b*) *lend money to a person otherwise unconnected with the company to enable him to purchase its shares;*
(*c*) *hold shares of another company;*
(*d*) *be appointed sole director of another company;*
(*e*) *be appointed liquidator of another company.*

QUESTION B18

Henry is the managing director of a company which has defaulted in payment of interest on a bank loan secured by a floating charge on the undertakings and assets. He has just had a telephone call from an accountant who said that the bank was appointing him to act as receiver and that he would be arriving later in the day. Henry has to break the news to his colleagues:

(a) Peter, the chairman, says 'I suppose we just have to do nothing except answer his questions when he puts them to us. It's up to him to ask for information.'
(b) Paul, the marketing manager but not a director, says 'I can't afford to be out of a job. As this one has gone I'd better look for another.'

(c) Charles, the company secretary, says 'Oh well, I'd better get on with the agenda and papers for next week's board meeting.'

Is each assumption correct?

QUESTION B19

Gee Ltd has an issued and fully paid share capital consisting of 100,000 £1 ordinary shares and 10,000 9% £1 cumulative preference shares. The class rights are set out in the articles of association. Paul and Tom, who hold all the ordinary shares and 8,000 of the preference shares, have decided to alter the articles so that the dividend on the preference shares shall no longer be cumulative and the rate shall be reduced to 6% pa.

Advise James, who holds the remaining 2,000 preference shares and opposes the proposals.

QUESTION B20

Zed, a limited company, has an authorised share capital of £100,000 in £1 ordinary shares of which 60,000 have been issued and are fully paid. The company intends:

(a) to cancel the 40,000 unissued shares;
(b) to repay in cash 50p per share to the holders of the 60,000 issued shares.

What is the procedure for effecting each of these changes? The company's articles of association are in the form of *Table A*.

QUESTION B21

If a company issues a prospectus inviting applications for shares in the company and the prospectus states that application will be made for permission for the shares to be dealt in on a stock exchange, what provision is made by CA 1948, with a view to protecting persons who apply for shares, against the possibility of the application for permission not being made, or, having been made, being refused?

QUESTION B22

George intends to lend £10,000 to a company whose principal assets are a freehold factory (which is already mortgaged to the bank), plant and vehicles and various current assets. The company has offered George as security a floating charge over its undertaking and assets.

(*a*) *To which assets will the floating charge apply?*
(*b*) *What disadvantages and risks does this type of security present to a lender?*

QUESTION B23

Explain the effect of the rule that prohibits a company from providing financial assistance towards the purchase of or subscription for its own shares and the exceptions to this rule.

QUESTION B24

Wye Plc, a public quoted company, has made a take-over bid for all the issued share capital of Tweed Plc.

Jack, a shareholder in Tweed Plc, opposes the bid as he considers that the price offered for his shares is inadequate. He discovers that Wye Plc is buying shares on the Stock Exchange at above the bid price and also that the directors of Tweed Plc, who recommend the bid, have been offered a higher price for their own shares.

Discuss the legal and other sanctions available to Jack.

QUESTION B25

Ibbotson was appointed by debenture holders to act as receiver of the undertaking and assets of a company which were subject to a floating charge given as security for the debentures. He has so far kept the business going and has retained the company's employees in service. It is becoming clear however that if the business is to be carried on the company will have to raise additional working capital by a bank loan (if this can be arranged). The alternative courses open are to look for a purchaser of the business as a going concern or to terminate its contracts with suppliers and customers and close it down.

Comment on the legal aspects of these three possible courses as they will affect Ibbotson and the company. (Under the terms of the debentures the receiver is the agent of the company and not of the debenture holders.)

QUESTION B26

A prospectus was issued to the public offering for subscription shares in a company. Having considered the prospectus, a person submitted an application for shares, and was in due course allotted the number of shares for which he had applied. Very soon thereafter he became aware that a part of the prospectus which had influenced him in his decision to apply for shares amounted to a material misrepresentation of fact.

Indicate three courses which may be open to the aggrieved person with a view to obtaining a remedy.

QUESTION B27

Porter Ltd is a trading company. A and B, the two directors, each hold 40% of the ordinary share capital. The remainder is held by D. A also holds debentures issued by Porter Ltd redeemable on 1 Jan. 1985. A wishes to dispose of his shares and debentures. B and D are anxious to help A, but do not wish control of Porter Ltd to pass into other hands. The following schemes are proposed:

(a) Porter Ltd will raise the necessary funds and purchase the shares and debentures for cash;

OR

(b) B will arrange a private loan so that he may purchase A's shares and debentures. Porter Ltd will guarantee the loan to B;

OR

(c) Porter Ltd will raise funds and lend them to D so that he may purchase A's shares and debentures.

Advise Porter Ltd on the legality of these three schemes and on the enforceability of the proposed guarantees.

QUESTION B28

How may membership of a company (a) be acquired and (b) cease? Make it clear when membership commences and when it is no longer effective.

QUESTION B29

Alma Co. Ltd has 20,000 £1 ordinary shares of which 5,000 have been issued. The company also has 5,000 issued £1, 10% cumulative preference shares. The following are alternative circumstances:

(a) the company proposes to reduce the dividend on the preference shares from 10% to 5%;
(b) the company proposes to issue the remaining ordinary shares to the existing ordinary shareholders;
(c) the company proposes to pay off the preference shares at par.

Advise Henry, who holds 1,000 preference shares and objects to all the proposals.

QUESTION B30

What is the purpose and effect of a 'floating charge' and in which documents or document would you expect to find such a charge created?

QUESTION B31

Bridge Ltd has a share capital of £20,000 divided into 20,000 £1 shares of which 5,000 have been issued.

The company is now in financial difficulties and wishes to raise some additional capital.

Advise the company in the following alternative circumstances:

(*a*) *the directors propose to issue 15,000 shares at 80p each;*
(*b*) *the directors propose to issue 25,000 shares at £1.20p each.*

QUESTION B32

Explain in what circumstances and how a receiver and manager for debenture holders can be appointed.

QUESTION B33

Your client Brown has lent £20,000 to A Ltd on the security of a debenture. The debenture gives a floating charge on the whole of the undertaking and assets of the company including its goodwill. To date, the company has complied with the terms of the debenture including the provisions about payment of interest. However, your client has learnt that various creditors who are owed a substantial sum by the company are now threatening to take legal action for recovery of the sums due to them. It is also understood that the landlord is threatening proceedings for recovery of outstanding rent due under the terms of the lease of the company's business premises.

What are the provisions of the Companies Acts concerning the need for registration of a floating charge? What action would you advise your client to take to enforce his security?

QUESTION B34

(a) The Companies Act empowers a company to alter or add to its articles by special resolution.

What limitations, if any, does the law place on the exercise of this power?

(b) The shares of Zed Ltd are all of one class. Its articles provide that dividends shall be paid in proportion to the amounts paid up on each holder's shares, but that bonus shares shall be issued in proportion to the nominal value of the shares held. John and Paul held partly paid up shares in Zed Ltd. When dividends were declared, each received only a proportion of the full dividend; but when bonus shares were issued, each was treated as favourably as a fully paid up shareholder.

The directors of Zed Ltd now propose to put a resolution before the company in general meeting to amend the articles. The amendment will provide that both cash dividends and bonus shares are to be distributed in proportion to the amounts paid up on shares. Their reason for this proposal is that the existing provision in the articles is unfair to fully paid up shareholders.

Advise John and Paul, who wish to challenge this proposed alteration of the articles.

QUESTION B35

Anthony and Charles were the controlling members of a private company each holding ordinary shares carrying one vote per share. There was only one other member, Fred, whose holding consisted mainly of preference shares carrying restricted voting rights. The company was in fact managed by directors none of whom held or were required by the articles to hold shares. In accordance with a power in the articles and with the support of the directors, Anthony and Charles resolved to issue further capital to themselves in the form of a bonus issue of preference shares. The essential purpose of this scheme was to dilute the voting strength of Fred on those occasions when Fred's shares gave him voting rights. At a general meeting an ordinary resolution to implement the scheme was passed by the voting strength of Anthony and Charles despite the protests of Fred.

Advise Fred, who claims:

(*i*) *that the scheme constitutes a variation of his class rights;*
(*ii*) *that he is entitled to relief under s. 75 CA 1980;*
(*iii*) *that Anthony and Charles as majority shareholders are subject to restraints imposed by common law and equity when voting at a general meeting to implement the proposed scheme.*

QUESTION C1

Thames Ltd is a company engaged in the manufacture of electrical switchgear. James, a director of the company, offered to sell to the company a quantity of copper rod which he knew was required. The board resolved to accept this offer but it was subsequently discovered that the price paid was very much higher than the current market price and that James had made a substantial profit on the transaction.

(*a*) *Can James be made to hand over his profit?*
(*b*) *Does it make any difference whether or not James attended and voted at the board meeting which accepted his offer?*

QUESTION C2

Harry is the company secretary of Wye Ltd. In the past he has been allowed to order stationery and office furniture and equipment but no single item has ever cost more than £200. Recently he ordered a computer and the company has received an invoice for £25,000. The board does not wish to proceed with the purchase.

Discuss.

QUESTION C3

The directors of Getrich Supermarkets Plc, a quoted company, have established a substantial business. They have been approached by their principal competitor whose business has been suffering from their competition and who are willing to sell at a low price. The directors knew that this would give the opportunity to combine the two businesses in such a way that together they would have a very strong hold on the supermarket business in their town and that the whole concern could then be sold on favourable terms to a national chain. The directors continued the negotiations for both these transactions without making any announcement of their intentions. As they saw an opportunity to make personal profits they proceeded to buy as many of the shares of the Getrich Supermarket Plc as they could obtain. Ultimately, the whole negotiations were satisfactorily completed and the shares were sold by the directors for three times the price they paid for them.

Are there any remedies available against the directors of Getrich Supermarkets Plc?

QUESTION C4

(*a*) *Explain the effect of the rule in Royal British Bank v Turquand (1856).*

(*b*) Harry, a director of Ribble Ltd, has entered into various contracts purporting to act on behalf of that company which its board wishes to repudiate. *Does it may any difference whether or not the outside traders to whom the orders were given inspected the memorandum and articles of association of Ribble Ltd?*

QUESTION C5

Henry is a minority shareholder in Yellor Plc, a company registered with articles of association in the form of *Table A*.

(a) Last year one of the employees of the company was convicted of stealing property belonging to the company and was put on probation. A general meeting instructed the directors to bring proceedings to recover the value of the property stolen but they refused to do so.

(b) The directors have diverted to themselves valuable contracts which were obtained for the company. They subsequently disclosed this action to a general meeting of the company which approved it by passing an ordinary resolution. The directors voted in favour of this resolution in respect of their own shares.

Can Henry bring proceedings successfully either personally or on behalf of the company in respect of either of these matters?

QUESTION C6

Alfred, Bernard and Charles are the directors of Private Ltd in which they own equally all the issued shares. Bernard and Charles have threatened to remove Alfred from office at the next board meeting if he continues to allege that Bernard and Charles are diverting business from Private Ltd to another company with which they are associated.

Advise Alfred.

QUESTION C7

The directors of Growkwik Plc have power to allot unissued but authorised capital of the company. They have used this power to allot all the company's unissued capital to friends at par although the current stock exchange quotation for the company's existing shares is at a higher price. The friends have agreed to share with the directors any resulting profits from selling their shares, and to vote as the directors wish in the event of a take-over bid being made for the company.

Discuss.

QUESTION C8

How far should an outsider dealing with a company make enquiries to ascertain that the appointment of a director with whom he is negotiating has been properly made, and what statutory provisions give the outsider protection in such circumstances?

QUESTION C9

The directors of Dozy Ltd have not called an Annual General Meeting of the company for nearly two years and a shareholders' committee has been formed. It wishes to call a meeting in order to remove the directors.

Advise the committee how they may proceed to call a general meeting or to have one called.

QUESTION C10

John and Harry are directors of White Plc, and they are negotiating for the sale of the whole of its undertakings to Blue Plc. It has not yet been decided whether to proceed by selling the assets of White Plc to Blue Plc as a going concern and then putting White Plc into liquidation, or by arranging for Blue Plc to make a bid for the shares of White Plc. John has a written service agreement with five years still to run, but Harry has no formal contract of service.

(*a*) *Will the choice of method affect the payment to John and Harry of compensation for loss of office?*
(*b*) *What must be done to comply with the Companies Act 1948 before any payment of such compensation may be made?*

QUESTION C11

Recent accounts of a private limited company reveal an accelerating deterioration in the cash flow which, if not reversed in the near future, could render the company unable to pay its trade creditors. The directors are, however, optimistic about the future.

Discuss the position of the directors if their optimism is unfounded and the company is subsequently wound up and is found to be insolvent.

QUESTION C12

Smith, who has a small shareholding in a public company, is very critical of the financial policy of the directors in various respects. At the forthcoming Annual General Meeting he would like (i) to put questions to the directors, (ii) to move a resolution criticising the directors' past decisions and also instructing them as to how they should proceed in future, and (iii) to oppose the re-election of those directors who are retiring by rotation unless satisfactory undertakings are given by the board as to future policy. The articles of the company are on all material points similar to *Table A*.

Can Smith do these things and if so what rules of procedure must he observe?

QUESTION C13

Exe Ltd has changed its articles by inserting a directors' share qualification clause. John, an existing director with a service contract which still has two years to run, has failed to acquire the necessary qualification shares.

Advise John.

QUESTION C14

X Ltd's principal object is to carry on the business of house-builders. The objects clause also authorises the company to enter into transactions incidental to that object; there is nothing else in the objects clause which is material here. The articles are in the form of *Table A*. Burnaby, who is an architect, has carried out a substantial amount of design work for the company on the instructions of Wright, one of its directors and the principal shareholder. Burnaby has just learnt that X Ltd is about to go into a creditors' voluntary winding up and is unlikely to be able to pay its creditors more than 25p in the £1 of its debts. Burnaby is a substantial but not the only creditor.

Advise him.

QUESTION C15

Alpha Ltd manufactures car electrical equipment, including car batteries. The articles of association contain an article which reads: 'The business of the company shall be managed by the directors who may exercise all such powers of the company as are not, by the Act or by these regulations, required to be exercised by the company in general meeting.'

Some of the employees in the battery works have contracted lead poisoning, which has resulted in adverse press publicity. At a general meeting of the company last year the shareholders resolved that the company should reduce its involvement in the manufacture of car batteries but, despite this resolution, the board of directors has decided to acquire additional capacity for the manufacture of batteries.

Discuss.

QUESTION C16

The fully paid share capital of Forth Ltd was held equally by the only three members, namely Mac, his wife Sheena, and Ewan. They were also the directors of the company. Three months ago Mac and Sheena were killed in a motor accident. Ewan has continued to run the company but, lacking financial expertise, has incurred heavy losses and feels that the company may have to be wound up. He has heard that he may be in danger of becoming personally liable for the company's debts.

Advise Ewan.

QUESTION C17

State, in your own words, the substance of the three propositions that were laid down in the case of the City Equitable Fire Insurance Co as to the skill and diligence required of a director.

QUESTION C18

What do you understand by the following terms:

(*a*) *quasi-loan,*
(*b*) *connected person,*
(*c*) *shadow director?*

QUESTION C19

Harold, a director of Wye Plc, has a written service agreement for ten years with six years unexpired. He receives remuneration of £7,500 pa. Recently he has had a serious disagreement with Peter, the managing director, because he has alleged that Peter has been misappropriating the funds of the company.

The company secretary has informed Harold that a special notice of resolution to remove him from office has been given to the company.

Advise Harold.

QUESTION C20

Sandra is employed as a secretary in the taxation department of a large firm of accountants who are the auditors of Mammoth Ltd, a public quoted company. Sandra's husband, Herbert, owned a large number of shares in Mammoth Ltd. Last week, whilst Sandra was having lunch with Arthur, an accountant who works in the audit department of the same firm, he told her that the unpublished accounts of Mammoth Ltd showed a considerably lower trading profit than would have been expected from current market trends. Arthur knew that Herbert owned shares in Mammoth Ltd. Sandra passed on the information to Herbert. Herbert had recently incurred large gambling debts and was being pressed for payment. After receiving the information from Sandra, Herbert sold his shares in Mammoth Ltd and applied the proceeds in paying his gambling debts.

Discuss the criminal liabilities (if any) of the parties.

QUESTION C21

Ernest has never been appointed the managing director of Wharfe Ltd but he has acted in that capacity for several years. In his capacity as managing director he has recently negotiated with a national distributor the purchase of a substantial quantity of goods on extended credit.

What obligation is there upon the national distributor to enquire into Ernest's authority and the company's capacity to contract?

QUESTION C22

A shareholder wishes to propose at the next Annual General Meeting of Goldplate Ltd that the company's head office in the West End of London be sold and replaced by less expensive premises. The directors have instructed the company secretary not to place this resolution on the agenda.

Advise the shareholder.

QUESTION C23

The *Companies Act 1980* has introduced the principle that directors shall have regard in the performance of their functions to the interests of the company's employees in general as well as the interests of its members.

What is the significance of this change?

QUESTION C24

When preparing accounts for J & J Ltd you are of the opinion that the company appears to be insolvent at the date of the balance sheet. You advise John, the managing director, and his wife Jill, also a director but who takes no active part in the management of the company, that the company should call a meeting of creditors unless there has been an improvement in the company's financial situation.

(*a*) *What risks does each run if they ignore your advice?*
(*b*) *What information would persuade you that the company is now solvent?*

QUESTION C25

(*a*) *What relationships disqualify an auditor from appointment as auditor to a company?*
(*b*) *Explain* (*i*) *the principal duties of an auditor, and* (*ii*) *the powers he has been granted by statute to discharge such duties.*

QUESTION D1

The notice issued to convene the AGM of X Ltd gave the necessary particulars of ordinary business and as special business set out the text of a special resolution to be proposed to alter the articles of association by increasing the limit on the directors' borrowing powers from £50,000 to £100,000. The articles of association of X Ltd prescribe a quorum for general meetings of three members personally present. There are only three members, A, B and C, each of whom holds one third of the issued ordinary shares. At the meeting A proposes (i) that the special resolution should be amended to set the new limit on borrowing at £75,000 and (ii) that it should require the directors to invite shareholders to subscribe for debentures before borrowing from outside sources. B, who is the chairman of the meeting, refuses to put either amendment to the vote although neither B nor C has any objection to the substance of either amendment. A then leaves the meeting in a rage and B and C pass the special resolution in its original form.

Advise A whether (i) the chairman's refusal of his amendments and (ii) the special resolution as passed are valid.

QUESTION D2

P, who holds 100 shares of a public company (whose issued ordinary share capital is one million shares), is very dissatisfied with the performance of the directors. He has given special notice to the company of his intention to move at the forthcoming AGM a resolution under *s. 184 CA 1948* to remove the managing director from office. He has now received a letter in reply from the secretary to inform him that the board declines to include his resolution in the notice to be issued to shareholders to convene the meeting. No reasons for this decision are given.

Advise P of his legal rights.

QUESTION D3

Z Ltd, a partly owned subsidiary of Y Ltd, has for many years owned a number of freehold properties which are shown in the accounts at values equal to acquisition costs with a note that the directors believe that their current values may be substantially in excess of book value, but no revaluation has so far been found necessary. One of the properties has recently been sold at book value. James, who is a small shareholder of Z, is outraged at the sale and considered that the directors who represented Y Ltd should be held accountable for the loss which he believes they have caused to the company by the sale.

Has he any remedy? Would it affect your answer if the sale had been made to a company whose sole beneficial owner is one of the directors?

QUESTION D4

George is the holder of 20% of the issued shares of a family company of which his late father was once chairman and managing director. The company did badly during his father's last years; at his death the company owed George's father about £20,000 which was money which the father had lent to keep the company going. It was not possible at his father's death for the company to repay the loan. George, who was sole executor, agreed with his cousin Henry, who took over the management of the company's business, that the loan should be repaid when the company was in a position to do so or, if not previously repaid, 10 years after his father's death. In the five years since then the company has prospered greatly but Henry says that it cannot yet spare the cash in order to repay the loan. Meanwhile a large part of the profits (before directors' remuneration) are being taken by Henry under a commission formula in his service agreement as managing director and no dividends have been paid. The other shareholders support Henry. George would like (i) to obtain repayment of the loan and (ii) to receive some dividends.

Has he any means to enforce these demands?

QUESTION D5

The articles of association of a company repeated the provisions contained in *Table A* of the first schedule to the *Companies Act 1948* relating to number of directors, appointment of additional directors, appointment of a managing director and rotation of directors. The number of directors had been fixed at not less than three and not more than ten.

The board had consisted of the chairman, the managing director and three others, each of whom also held whole-time executive appointments with the company, but since the last annual general meeting the board had appointed as additional directors three other persons who also held whole-time appointments with the company. All the eight persons concerned had some years to go before reaching the age limit.

Assuming all were willing and eligible to continue, how many directors would be due to come up for re-election at the next following annual general meeting? Show your reasoning.

QUESTION D6

A property company owns two major assets: Site A valued in its books at £200,000 and Site B valued in the books at £300,000. The directors propose to revalue Site B at £350,000 on the advice of a professional valuer, to sell Site A for £150,000 to improve the cash position and to pay a dividend of £20,000. There are no other profits or reserves available for distribution as dividend.

Is the directors' scheme legally permissible?

QUESTION D7

Dee Ltd is the holding company of several partly-owned subsidiaries, all of which have old-fashioned complex capital structures comprising many types of shares carrying widely varying rights. Frequent dealings in these shares are causing severe administrative difficulties in paying dividends and registering transfers.

Advise Dee Ltd as to the manner and means in which it can arrange a simplification of the capital structure of the group in order to obviate these difficulties.

QUESTION D8

Growth Plc has recently offered to acquire all the issued share capital of Dozy Plc that it does not already own. The offer is of one ordinary share of Growth for every one share of Dozy held by its members. The offer document issued by Moneybank, the merchant bank acting for Growth, states that Moneybank is prepared to pay £5 cash for every five shares of Growth, which any offeree may wish to sell; but this cash offer is available for one month only. The offer is conditional upon acceptance by the holders of not less than 90% of the shares for which the offer is made and states that if declared unconditional, *s. 209(1) CA 1948* will be applied to acquire the shares of non-acceptors on the same basis of share exchange as mentioned above. Thomas, a shareholder of Dozy, is reluctant to accept the offer. He has been told that in the weeks just before its offer was announced Growth was buying shares of Dozy in the market at prices up to £1.05 each.

Advise him.

QUESTION D9

Esk Ltd incurred trading losses during each of the four years of its existence and its net assets only represent one half of the nominal value of its issued share capital. In the fifth year it made a profit which the directors now wish to distribute as dividend.

Discuss. Would your answer be different if Esk were a public limited company?

QUESTION D10

John has recently become the registered holder of ordinary shares in Traders Ltd inherited from his father. He finds that although the company has substantial assets it is not making adequate profits and for some years has not paid dividends. The company is managed by working directors who merely hold a small number of qualification shares and draw substantial remuneration for their inefficient services. They are content: John is not.

Advise John.

QUESTION D11

(*a*) *What is a committee of inspection and by whom are its members appointed?*
(*b*) Charles (a creditor) attended a regular meeting of a committee of inspection last week. On the basis of information just received he considers that the committee should be immediately reconvened as a matter of urgency; the liquidator however does not agree. *Can Charles get his way?*

QUESTION D12

Property Ltd is the lessor of a factory let to Trading Ltd under a seven year lease at a rent of £10,000 p.a. Trading recently went into creditors' voluntary winding up: it has ceased to trade, the factory is empty and the company is said to have no realisable assets.

Advise Property as to the courses of action open to the liquidator of Trading and of any action which Property might take to mitigate its prospective loss of rental income.

QUESTION D13

Michael and Norman transferred their partnership business to a limited company of which they were appointed sole directors and of which the share capital was allotted to them in equal shares in satisfaction of the purchase consideration. Norman's son Oswald served his apprenticeship with the company, and, on satisfactorily completing his training, he was allotted 100 shares by the company and appointed to the board of directors. Oswald and Norman have now passed a resolution removing Michael as a director.

Advise Michael.

QUESTION D14

A shareholder of a public company has written to the Department of Trade to make a detailed complaint of alleged irregularities in the conduct of the company's overseas subsidiaries. Nothing of these matters can be learnt from the company's published group accounts. The Department has written to the company requiring it to produce to the Department various specified classes of documents which may throw light on these matters.

What are the legal powers of the Department to investigate in this way? Can the company refuse to comply with the Department's request?

QUESTION D15

Some of the shareholders of Gamma Ltd have written to the Department of Trade requesting an investigation into the company's affairs on the ground that the directors are in breach of various provisions of the Companies Acts.

What are the powers of the Department in a situation of this kind?

QUESTION D16

R Ltd, now in liquidation, has the following debts:

(a) £30,000 overdraft with the bank secured by a legal mortgage on the company's premises (duly registered); the premises are worth £30,000;
(b) £17,000 owing to Smith, a full-time working director. He lent the company £15,000 on the security of a floating charge (duly registered) on its assets. £1,000 is due to him as directors' fees and £1,000 as salary;
(c) £3,000 in wages to employees;
(d) £2,000 in dividends declared but not yet paid;
(e) £50,000 to trade creditors.

The company's assets (including the premises) are worth £50,000.

In what order will the claims of creditors rank for payment?

QUESTION D17

(*a*) *State the three occasions when 'special notice' is required of a resolution to be proposed at a company's general meeting.*
(*b*) *What requirements must be fulfilled to pass validly:*
  (*i*) *such a resolution, and*
  (*ii*) *a 'special resolution'?*

QUESTION D18

Fine Arts Ltd has three shareholders, each of whom owns one third of the share capital. Two of them, A and B, are directors and manage the business; C retired some years ago. C is indignant to learn that A and B have decided to sell for £50,000 a painting which C considers is worth at least £100,000; he considers that it is highly incompetent of A and B to sell now at this price rather than wait for a rise in the market.

Can C prevent the sale? Would it make any difference if the purchaser was a firm of art dealers in which A and B were sleeping partners?

QUESTION D19

(*a*) *In relation to a petition for the winding up of a company by the court, what are the three circumstances in which a company will be deemed to be unable to pay its debts?*

(*b*) *Explain the statement that the 'just and equitable' ground for a winding up by the court need not be of the same kind as other grounds specified in the Act and give two examples of circumstances in which the winding-up has been ordered on the 'just and equitable' ground.*

QUESTION D20

Henry has a claim against Q Ltd for £500, the agreed price of goods supplied. As he has been unable to obtain payment he is considering presenting a petition to the court for the compulsory winding up of the company. He has been told that his petition will be opposed

(a) by the company which asserts that the goods supplied were not of the quality required by the contract and are worthless, and

(b) by George, a director of the company, to whom the company owes £5,000 in unpaid director's fees.

Advise Henry of his prospects of success in his peitition.

QUESTION D21

On 1 Feb. this year you were appointed liquidator of a company in a creditors' voluntary winding up. Your investigations reveal the following transactions:

(a) On 1 Jan. last year the company borrowed £2,000 from one of its directors on the security of a floating charge (duly registered) on its stock in trade. The current value of the stock in trade is £3,000.

(b) On 30 Sep. two years ago the managing director deposited with the company's bank as security for its overdraft the title deeds of his house. On 30 Sep. last year the company paid off its overdraft and the title deeds were released by the bank.
(c) On 31 Oct. last year the company paid £2,000 to its largest trade creditor, who had threatened to sue for the amount owing to it.

What action (if any) can you take as liquidator in respect of each of these transactions?

QUESTION D22

X Ltd already holds all the issued ordinary shares of Y Ltd and is planning to acquire the preference shares of Y Ltd from minority shareholders by offering ordinary shares of X in exchange for preference shares of Y. But some holders of the preference shares may not wish to accept the proposed exchange.

What alternative methods of effecting the exchange so as to obtain all the preference shares of Y are open to X and what are the comparative advantages and disadvantages of each?

QUESTION D23

Explain the concept of 'preferential debts' for the purposes of the Companies Acts and state the circumstances in which it is relevant.

QUESTION D24

What is the effect of a company going into liquidation on:
(i) the powers of the directors;
(ii) the contract of employment of its staff;
(iii) the legal title to its assets;
(iv) the transfer of its shares;
(v) a debenture issued by the company and secured by a floating charge;
(vi) an impending action against the company for debt instituted by a creditor.

QUESTION D25

The directors of Pork Pies Ltd have sold the company's business for £20,000 to another company, Rashers Ltd, of which they are also directors and majority shareholders. The company's net assets are valued at £50,000. Squealer, a shareholder in Pork Pies Ltd, claims that the directors have acted improperly and ought to compensate the company for any loss. He has attempted to requisition a meeting of the shareholders to propose the removal of the directors under *s. 184 CA 1948* but has been thwarted in his attempts by the directors.

Discuss and, in particular, consider whether there are any further measures Squealer can take against the directors.

QUESTION D26

Bert Botchit is the managing director of Botchit's Burton brewery, a family company founded by Bert's grandfather. His fellow directors are his wife, Bertha, and son, Brian.

Owing to the increased public demand for real ale, United Gassy Beers, a large beverage conglomerate, has just taken over Botchit's Brewery. UGB invites you, as a professional adviser, to investigate Botchit's rather chaotic affairs. You discover the following:

(a) Bertha Botchit has just granted a loan of £20,000 out of company assets to her dancing partner, Byron, to open a disco-dancing studio. There is no note of this, nor do her fellow directors know of its existence. Byron has also arranged a contract for his dance studio to be supplied with Botchit's beers at most favourable prices.

(b) Brian has persuaded his father to buy a Maserati out of company funds and lease it back to him for £1 per week. He has also used the company's Harridge's account card to buy expensive presents for his girl-friend. He has reluctantly agreed to pay back the £5,000 owing, but says that he cannot do it until next year. He also argues that part of the outstanding balance was spent by him on business suits and on food and wine for a reception held for the directors of UGB.

What are the legal implications of these transactions?

QUESTION D27

The *Companies Act 1948* provides a right to disclaim onerous property.

(*a*) *By whom, with what consent, and within what time limits may such a right be exercised?*

(*b*) *In respect of what types of property may it be exercised?*

(*c*) *What is the purpose of the grant of such right?*

(*d*) *What rights has the person who suffers loss by the disclaimer?*

QUESTION D28

What does the Companies Act 1948 provide as to:

(*a*) *maintaining records of proceedings at meetings;*
(*b*) *the effect of such records; and*
(*c*) *inspection and copies of such records?*

Ignore the provisions for penalties and the provisions particularly related to meetings held in the course of winding-up.

QUESTION D29

Following an industrial rationalisation scheme Wye Holdings Ltd was formed to acquire the ordinary share capitals of several companies. The companies have a wide variety of preference share issues with complex rights and the registration of transfers and the payment of dividends is causing severe administration difficulty.

Advise Wye Holdings Ltd how it can arrange a simplification of the capital structure of the group.

QUESTION D30

Arnold and Benjamin have for many years been the sole shareholders and directors of Careless Ltd. The company is now insolvent and in voluntary liquidation.

State what action a liquidator should take in respect of the following:

(*a*) *notification of his appointment;*
(*b*) *the directors' remuneration has never been approved by a general meeting but only a directors' meeting;*
(*c*) *the directors, only three months ago, gave a debenture containing a floating charge on the company's book debts to one of the creditors.*

QUESTION D31

Z Ltd is in voluntary liquidation. It is a private company and there is only one director, namely Jones. Jones has disappeared but the liquidator has information suggesting that he can easily be traced.

The liquidator has discovered that Jones purchased goods on behalf of the company but when writing up the company's books showed the goods at the full price and took for himself the discount which he obtained when making the purchases. The company owes £6,000 to Money Bank, being a sum lent to cover the wages paid to the company's six employees in the month prior to the resolution for the winding up. £4,000 is due to the Inland

Revenue in respect of unpaid PAYE deductions over the two years before the commencement of the winding up.

It rapidly becomes clear that the company became insolvent some months ago as the result of several risky speculative transactions to which it was committed by Jones. Jones had guaranteed the company's overdraft with Money Bank Ltd but four months before the resolution for the winding up arranged for company funds to be used to pay off the overdraft instead of paying trade creditors and obtained a release from the guarantee.

In what order should the liquidator pay the company's debts? What action if any can he take to increase the assets available for distribution?

QUESTION D32

Describe the following, giving examples:

(*a*) *a reconstruction,*
(*b*) *an amalgamation,*
(*c*) *an arrangement or compromise.*

Answers

ANSWER A1

A company is a separate person from its members even if all its issued shares are beneficially owned by one individual: *Salomon v Salomon & Co Ltd* (*1897*). The assets of a company are its property in which a shareholder has no legal interest: *Macaura v Northern Assurance Co Ltd* (*1925*). On a simple application of these principles Jones cannot compel the company, which is not a party to the contract, to perform Smith's contract. But the veil of incorporation will be lifted to prevent a person (Smith) using it in a fraudulent or improper manner: *Gilford Motor Co Ltd v Horne* (*1933*). The facts are taken from *Jones v Lipman* (*1962*) where an order was made for specific performance by the company which the court described as a 'mask which he holds before his face ... a device and a sham'. Smith cannot, therefore, keep the house in the company and merely pay Jones damages: the court is likely to recognise the artificial nature of the transfer to the company, lift the veil of incorporation, and order the conveyance of the house to Jones.

Jones should be advised accordingly.

ANSWER A2

As all three ladies intend to take part in the *management*, a limited partnership is not practicable. They can do so either as partners or directors (but not merely as members) of a limited company. Of these two alternatives only a limited company would permit them to avoid *personal liability*. Of the two types of limited companies, public and private, a private company is appropriate unless it is intended to raise funds from the public, which seems unlikely. On the other hand a limited company is required to prepare and to file at the Companies Registry a memorandum and articles of association, annual return, and other documents. It must also maintain registers some of which are open to public inspection. A partnership has the advantage that its constitution and affairs will remain *confidential*. One of the advantages of incorporation of a company limited by shares is the facility for transfer of the members' interests. In the case of a private limited company this freedom had to be limited by the inclusion in the articles of the company of some restriction on the transferability of the shares (usually a clause that the directors could refuse to register a transfer): *s. 28 CA 1948*. Now that this restriction is no longer essential (*s. 28* was repealed by *CA 1980*), the three ladies will be able to form a private limited company *and* have complete freedom to transfer their shares. It is not possible to transfer a partner's interest so as to admit the transferee to the partnership unless all the other partners consent.

Prior to *CA 1981*, one could not achieve both limited liability and secrecy. The accounts of all limited companies, since *CA 1967*, had to be filed with the Registrar of Companies and therefore available to the general public. However, under *CA 1981* 'small companies' as defined by the Act (effective in this respect from 15 Jun. 1982) need only file a modified balance sheet (giving main headings and little detail), and no profit and loss account or directors' report need be filed. There is therefore no longer any point in sacrificing limited liability by using an unlimited company or partnership to avoid filing accounts (although full accounts in accordance with the Act must still be prepared for members).

ANSWER A3

A company has power to carry on such business as is covered by an express object (or is incidental thereto): *Ashbury Railway Carriage & Iron Co Ltd v Riche* (1875). Unless the objects clause specifies restaurants as an object or contains a *Bell Houses* type of additional object it will be necessary to amend the objects clause under *s. 5 CA 1948* (which among other things permits extension of the clause to a business which can be *advantageously combined with the existing business*). The directors and their supporters with 82% of the votes can carry a special resolution for this purpose. If however the members who object hold at least 15% of the shares they can within 21 days take their objections to the court and the court has power to cancel or amend the alteration or, since *CA 1980*, to impose terms including, if it wishes, an order for the objectors' shares to be bought out.

If the existing business is being closed down, the alteration would not be within *s. 5* and could be opposed by a court application by *any* shareholder within 21 days, in which case, the court must refuse to sanction it.

CA 1981 introduces new rules on company and business names as from 26 Feb. 1982. Generally, no approval of a name need now be sought from the Registrar before a company formation or change of name. In practice the index kept by him will need to be checked because he will be able to order a change of name within 12 months if the name is too like an existing name. The change is effected by special resolution and becomes effective when an amended certificate is issued by the Registrar: *s. 24 CA 1981*. The Registry of Business Names is abolished, but if a company chooses to trade under a name other than its own (e.g. X Ltd trades as 'Good Food'), business letters, orders, invoices, receipts and written demands for payment must show the name of the proprietor and an address for service of documents. A notice must be prominently posted at the business premises to the same effect.

ANSWER A4

(*a*) A company has power (*s. 10 CA 1948*) to alter its articles of association by passing a special resolution and this power cannot be contracted out of. The power is however subject to certain restrictions, one of which is that the power may only be exercised if the alteration is *bona fide* for the benefit of the company as a whole and not for the advantage of the members who vote in favour of it: *Greenhalgh v Arderne Cinemas Ltd* (*1946*).

But it is well established (*Shuttleworth v Cox Bros & Co*

(*Maidenhead*) *Ltd* (*1927*)) that if the majority reasonably believe that an alteration of the articles will benefit the company it is no valid objection that some individual member thereby suffers hardship. Accordingly Patrick cannot prevent the alteration of the articles. Y Ltd has sufficient shares to give it the 75% majority required to pass a special resolution.

(*b*) If Patrick's appointment as managing director for life was effected only by the articles of association, he held his appointment on the basis that the company had statutory power to alter its articles and that he is not entitled to notice or to damages if in altering its articles it terminates his appointment. Patrick could not rely on the contract in the articles under *s. 20 CA 1948* to enforce this provision as that contract is only for the enforcement by members of members' rights: *Eley v Positive Government Security Life Assurance Co Ltd* (*1876*). Moreover, Patrick could be removed from his position as a director by passing only an ordinary resolution: *s. 184 CA 1948*. This would automatically terminate his appointment as managing director where *Table A* articles are adopted (*Article 107*). But if Patrick has a separate service agreement for a specified period or even for life the company, although its power to alter its articles is still unrestricted, is liable to pay damages for any breach of the agreement: *Southern Foundries* (*1926*) *Ltd v Shirlaw* (*1940*). It seems that a director may not always be regarded as an employee for the purposes of employment protection legislation: *Parsons v Parsons & Sons Ltd* (*1979*).

CA 1980 prohibits the inclusion in a director's contract of employment a term appointing him for a period in excess of five years, unless the term is first approved by the shareholders in general meeting: *s. 47 CA 1980*. A term appointing someone managing director for life would contravene this provision and the effect of the section would be to remove the offending clause and replace it with one entitling the company to dismiss the director on giving reasonable notice only. The Act is not retrospective however, and although *s. 47* was implemented in 1980 this was not done until 22 Dec. of that year. Therefore, *s. 47 CA 1980* probably does not apply. Patrick could therefore claim damages for dismissal on the basis of loss of his position for life.

ANSWER A5

It is likely that the company has power in its objects clause to sell its property, i.e. the hotels, and that the articles of association follow the model of *Table A Article 80* in giving the directors general authority to exercise the powers of the company in business transactions. If that is the position the proposal to sell the hotels is within the powers of the directors. The directors are of course bound to exercise their powers in good faith for the benefit of the company and not themselves. If challenged on this point the directors would have to make out a reasonable commercial case for the proposed sale.

As a general rule a company cannot do anything which is not expressly provided for in its objects clause or reasonably ancillary to those objects. Any such transactions would be *ultra vires* and void: *Ashbury Railway Carriage & Iron Co Ltd v Riche (1875)*.

In relation to gratuitous transactions, even if the company had an express power to make gifts this could only be exercised if reasonably incidental and beneficial to the company's business; *a fortiori*, the courts were reluctant to imply a power to make gifts. In *Parke v Daily News Ltd (1962)* the court refused to imply a power to make *ex gratia* redundancy payments to employees on the cessation of the company's business as such payments could not be reasonably incidental to the business of the company, nor beneficial to the company.

S. 74 CA 1980 provides that in the absence of an express power to make *ex gratia* redundancy payments to employees, there should be implied such a power which can be exercised notwithstanding that it is not in the best interests of the company. This effectively overrules the decision in *Parke v Daily News Ltd (1962)*.

The directors could therefore make the proposed redundancy payments to the employees under this provision as long as the payments are made from profits available for distribution defined in *s. 39 CA 1980*. If there is no specific authority in the memorandum for such gratuitous payments an ordinary resolution will be required; thus the minority shareholder may object to the payments but unless he can obtain the support of the majority he will be unsuccessful. If there is no specific authority in the memorandum, the directors may proceed whether or not the payments will benefit the company and do not then need the members' approval.

The directors could not award themselves payments as this would be in breach of their fiduciary duty not to put themselves in a position of conflict of interest and duty. Such breaches are usually capable of ratification by the shareholders in general meeting, but where the directors are diverting corporate property to themselves the position is not clear. The minority shareholder could claim that the directors are committing a fraud on the minority and obtain judgement against the directors on behalf of the company: *Daniels v Daniels (1978)*.

If as a result of the cessation of business the directors will lose their positions as directors, they may keep the payments subject to disclosure and approval by the shareholders: *s. 191 CA 1948*. (Compensation for loss of office provisions.)

Damages for breach of contract need not be disclosed in this way, but the redundancy payments are in excess of those provided for in their contracts.

The minority may object at the shareholder's meeting to these proposals but otherwise he has no right to interfere in management. If the directors are committing a fraud on the minority, a derivative action may be available to him.

It is unnecessary at this stage to consider whether Developer's scheme for conversion of hotels into offices is *ultra vires*. He might well have to amend the objects clause after securing control of the company, but it is unlikely that he would fit within the grounds for alteration outlined in *s. 5 CA 1948*.

ANSWER A6

Shares are freely transferable except to the extent that the articles of association impose any restriction. (Before *CA 1980* private companies had to include some restriction on the transfer of shares.)

Charles should consider the relevant articles. Do they give the directors a power in their discretion and without giving reasons to refuse to register any transfer of shares; or some narrower power, e.g. to refuse a transfer on specified grounds? If so, Charles may demand to know on what grounds the directors rely but not their reasons in detail.

If the directors have a power to refuse to register a transfer they are still required to consider any transfer sent in for registration, i.e. merely to ignore it is not a valid exercise of the power. It must be exercised within a reasonable time—or it lapses—and notice of the refusal must be given within two months of presentation of the transfer: *s. 78 CA 1948*. Finally, the refusal is valid only if the directors took their decision in the interests of the company and not to secure some personal advantage or to pursue a vendetta. But it will not be easy for Charles, on whom the burden of proof rests, to establish the motives of directors who need usually give no reasons for their decision.

If the directors have no power to refuse to register the transfer, Charles could obtain a court order to force the directors to place the transferee's name on the register.

On the second point Charles can only rely on the articles if they operate under *s. 20 CA 1948* as a contract between members on a matter affecting rights and obligation of members. In *Eley v Positive Government Security Life Assurance Co Ltd* (*1876*) a solicitor could not rely on the articles which provide that he should be a solicitor to the company since although he was a member this was not a membership matter. However, the transfer of shares is a membership matter. But is this a dispute between members? Directors as such are not required also to be members. But if articles require that the directors should hold qualification shares the directors must also be members and can be compelled under articles in this form to purchase the shares offered to them: *Rayfield v Hands* (*1960*), where the facts were similar on the essential points.

ANSWER A7

The only type of company which is exempt (*s. 47 CA 1967*) from the general requirement of delivering a signed copy of its accounts to the Companies Registry is an unlimited company which is neither the holding company nor the subsidiary of a limited company. If James and his sons are prepared to forgo the protection of limited liability in order to withhold the accounts from public inspection they may convert the company from limited to unlimited.

Application must be made to the Registrar of Companies (signed by a director or by the Secretary), having attached to it:

(a) the written consent to the changes of all members of the company or their agents;
(b) a statutory declaration by the directors that the signatories to the written consent are the entire membership or their agents;
(c) an amended copy of the memorandum and articles of association incorporating the changes appropriate to an unlimited company.

The Registrar issues a certificate of re-registration of the company as unlimited. The issue of this certificate makes the change effective. James could convert the company into a partnership or limited partnership—neither of which require disclosure of the accounts—but the question seems to be restricted to types of company not other types of business association.

CA 1981 eases the present disclosure burden on small private companies. If James does not wish to forgo limited liability as indicated above and his company qualifies as a 'small' company, as from 15 June 1982 it need only file a 'modified' balance sheet (containing the items shown as main headings in the formats prescribed by the Act)—no profit and loss account, no directors' report and only limited notes to the accounts. Full accounts will need to be prepared for the members but if James takes advantage of these filing exemptions, he will have all the secrecy he needs as the information which has to be filed is very limited in scope.

ANSWER A8

A company has power to enter into transactions covered by its express objects or incidental thereto. As this company's sole object is railway construction in England it is clear that railway modernisation in USA and supply of channel ferry equipment are both likely to be outside its capacity and *ultra vires*. An *ultra vires* contract is void and the directors (i) would be liable to make good to the company any loss it might sustain and (ii) could be restrained by injunction from committing the company to such contracts even if the members in general meeting approved what they had done or proposed to do: *Ashbury Railway Carriage & Iron Co Ltd v Riche* (*1875*) (where the facts were somewhat similar). Also, the directors risk liability to any outsider who suffers loss because of an *ultra vires* contract if they are in breach of warranty of authority.

The directors' problem might be solved by first altering the objects clause of its memorandum so as to permit the company to carry on business of this kind. The objects may be altered *inter alia* to include additional business which can be advantageously combined with the existing business and to enlarge the geographical area of its operations: *s. 5 CA 1948*. But the alteration must not be positively destructive of the original objects: *Re Cyclists Touring Club* (*1907*) or it will not be within *s. 5* and must be set aside by the court if any shareholder applies to the court within 21 days of the passing of the resolution. If, however, the alteration is within *s. 5* and the directors are able to carry the necessary special resolution to alter the objects at a meeting which they can convene for this purpose, there is still the risk that holders of at least 15% of the shares (or any class of shares) who did not vote in favour of the resolution may appeal to the court within 21 days: the court may cancel or modify the alteration or impose a compromise. *S. 5 CA 1948* cannot be used to ratify an *ultra vires* transaction.

A signed copy of the special resolution and of the memorandum as altered must be filed at the Companies Registry within the specified time limit.

If the directors did continue with the proposed new businesses without altering the objects any shareholder could apply to the court for a winding up of the company on the just and equitable ground because there has been a failure of the substratum of the company: *s. 222(f) CA 1948; Re German Date Coffee Co (1882).*

ANSWER A9

A company cannot enter into a contract before it has been incorporated. It is not an existing person with capacity to contract until that stage is reached. For the same reason a company cannot after incorporation ratify a contract made on its behalf before incorporation: *Kelner v Baxter (1866).*

Although the company will not be bound by a pre-incorporation contract, those who purport to contract on its behalf as its agents are liable for breach of the implied warranty of authority: *Kelner v Baxter; s. 9(2) ECA 1972* provides that any person purporting to contract on behalf of a non-existent company shall be personally liable on the contract. This is so even if the contract is expressed to be made by the company and not by its agents.

Similarly, there is doubt whether A and B could hold C to the contract if they made it on the non-existing company's behalf: *Newborne v Sensolid (Great Britain) Ltd (1954)*; but because of the wording of *s. 9* (on which, in this respect, there have been no case law decisions) it seems likely that the promoters could now sue the other party.

A and B could, of course, contract in their own names as principals and would then obviously be able to sue; but they would also be personally liable.

If therefore A and B accede to C's demand they will become personally liable on the contract. If C cannot be persuaded to wait until the company is formed, A and B could offer to enter into a contract with the declared intention of replacing it by a new contract to be entered into by the company after incorporation, and with provisions by which A and B could at their option terminate their contract with C if the company does not before the time for performance arrives enter into the proposed new contract with C. The initial contract would of course provide that A and B would be released from their contract when the replacement contract is made by the company after incorporation. Alternatively, A and B could abandon the formation and instead buy a ready-made company for the purpose.

ANSWER A10

A company is a separate legal entity from its shareholders and directors: *Salomon v Salomon & Co Ltd* (*1897*). Although it is a separate person it cannot physically act on its own thus; thus it is usual to delegate the control and management of the company's affairs to the directors. *Article 80* of *Table A* provides that the directors shall manage the company and exercise such powers as are not reserved for the shareholders either by the company's articles or the *Companies Acts 1948–1981*. As a general principle shareholders are not allowed to manage the company's affairs. Their control is limited to control over the directors by the appointment or dismissal of directors: *s. 184 CA 1948*; and alteration of the articles (perhaps restricting the directors' authority): *s. 10 CA 1948*.

In a small company the shareholders may also be the directors, in which case the formal distinction between control and ownership is blurred. In a larger company the directors may be members, but there is no legal obligation on them unless they are required by the articles to hold qualification shares. The larger the company the less the control (in percentage terms) any person is likely to have over the company. Certain powers may only be exercised by the shareholders in general meeting—i.e. exclusive powers, e.g. to alter the articles (*s. 10 CA 1948*) or to sanction a reduction of capital (*s. 66 CA 1948*). Other powers may be exercised simultaneously with the main organ of control—the board of directors. Finally, the shareholders may have default powers which they can exercise if the directors are unable or unwilling to act. Generally, these are very restricted. There is some debate concerning the 'shareholders' right' to litigate on behalf of the company where the directors are refusing to bring an action against a wrongdoer on behalf the company.

In *Marshall's Valve Gear Co Ltd v Manning Wardle & Co Ltd* (*1909*) the shareholders were allowed to initiate legal proceedings on behalf of the company when the directors failed to do so. In any case the shareholders may only act on behalf of the company when acting in a formal way—i.e. a resolution of the members in general meeting, either ordinary (50%) or special (75%). In all decided cases where the general meeting has been permitted to sue where the directors have refused to do so, the directors have had some personal motive for not wishing the company to sue: in the *Marshall's Valve Gear* case, the majority of the board had an interest in the concern they were refusing to sue.

Tutorial note

The question of how far the shareholders can control the way the board runs the company is known as the problem of 'division of powers' and depends essentially upon how the articles of a particular company divide the running of the company.

ANSWER A11

A company's power to enter into binding contracts is (as a basic principle) restricted to transactions within the scope of its objects clause or reasonably identical to such matters. Any other contracts are *ultra vires* the company and are void unless authorised by statute.

The most effectual safeguard now offered to a person entering into contracts with a company is afforded by *s. 9(1) ECA 1972* which provides that in favour of a person dealing in good faith with a company any transaction decided on by its directors shall be deemed to be within the capacity of the company in spite of any restriction contained in the memorandum and articles of association.

However, Norman is probably unable to rely on *s. 9(1)* because he has been dealing over these contracts with a single director (John). The other directors have permitted John to exercise the powers of a managing director but the contracts have not been approved at a board meeting. They are not therefore transactions decided on by the directors.

In allowing John to act as a managing director the other directors may have 'held out' John as having the authority to enter into contracts (as in *Freeman and Lockyer v Buckhurst Park Properties Ltd* (*1964*)) and the company might on that ground be estopped from denying that he has authority. It seems however that this principle of estoppel does not apply to an *ultra vires* contract: *British Mutual Banking Co v Charnwood Forest Rail Co* (*1887*).

Although *s. 180 CA 1948* provides that the acts of a director will be valid notwithstanding defects in his appointment or qualification, this only applies when there has been a purported appointment: *Morris v Kanssen* (*1946*); and when the director's action would be valid but for the defect of appointment, which is not the case here as the director acts *ultra vires*.

For these reasons Norman cannot enforce against the company the contracts negotiated with John. He may have a claim for damages against John for misrepresenting that he and the company had the power which they lacked: *West London Commercial Bank v Kitson* (*1883*)—i.e. an action for breach of an implied warranty of authority. This is one of a number of non-contractual remedies available to outsiders whose contracts turn out to be *ultra vires* and void, such as training and following property which still belongs to the outsider or relying on subrogation where the outsider's loan to the company has been used to pay *ultra vires* debts.

ANSWER A12

The memorandum and articles of association are by *s. 20 CA 1948* a contract binding as if executed under seal between the company and its members and between the members themselves. But it is a contract binding only in respect of rights and obligations of members; only members are bound and then only in respect of membership matters.

In *Eley v Positive Government Security Life Assurance Co Ltd* (*1876*) the articles provided that Eley, who was a member, should be employed as the company's solicitor (without any time limit being specified). It was held that Eley could not enforce the articles as a contract of employment because this was not a right of membership. But in *Salmon v Quin & Axtens Ltd* (*1909*) a managing director was able to enforce a power of veto over board decisions relying purely on the contract in the articles provided for in *s. 20 CA 1948*, even though this was a non-member's (i.e. an outsider's) right. In both these cases the plaintiff was a member but in the problem there is no indication that either Donald or Charles are members. If they could rely on *Salmon's Case* they must at least be members themselves.

However, where companies have in fact employed directors in the absence of an express agreement it has been held (*Re New British Iron Co ex parte Beckwith* (*1898*)) that a separate contract of service may be established by the parties' course of dealing with each other, i.e. implied from their conduct, which may include terms found in the articles. In effect the articles are not in such a case a contract but they offer evidence of what has been agreed in a separate contract between the parties. In *Beckwith's Case* the articles were referred to as evidence of the salary which the company had agreed to pay. In *Eley's Case*, however, the court refused (partly for technical reasons abolished by the subsequent repeal of the *s. 4 Statute of Frauds*) to treat the articles as evidence of an agreement to employ Eley indefinitely merely because his services had been used by the company for a time (i.e. there was no evidence of a contract separate from the articles).

The company will rely on *Eley's Case* and Donald will argue that the article in question and his long service are evidence of a contract to employ him to the age of 65. The court would have to decide which of the two conflicting precedents it prefers. If, as is probable, the court follows *Beckwith's Case* and holds that the contract binds the company until Donald is 65, damages will be payable for premature termination by his dismissal. Even if Donald cannot rely on the articles, he is entitled (apart from statutory compensation for 'unfair dismissal') to reasonable notice or salary (at not less than £10,000 pa) in lieu of notice.

The same principle applies to employer and employee. If Donald is subject to dismissal, Charles is entitled to resign (on reasonable notice). If Donald cannot be dismissed, Charles cannot resign.

ANSWER A13

A company can only do those things stated in its objects clause or ancillary to those objects—otherwise it is acting *ultra vires* and any such transaction is void: *Ashbury Railway Carriage & Iron Ltd v Riche* (*1875*). The bank will be unable to sue on the loan contract if it is *ultra vires* and void. The bank may however be able to trace its money into the company's hands unless the money can no longer be identified. *S. 9 ECA 1972* may apply to validate an *ultra vires* transaction if the bank was acting in good faith and the transaction was decided on by the directors. This latter requirement is complied with. Whether the bank has acted in good faith is a question of fact. If for example the bank manager had read the objects clause and knows the limits of the company's capacity he could hardly be acting in good faith. However, *s. 9 ECA 1972* assumes the creditor to be acting in good faith unless the company can prove lack of *bona fides*. This might be a difficult evidential problem for the company.

The question describes the other two objects as *subsidiary*. This probably is to be taken to mean that there is no independent object clause declaring all the clauses to be independent and not subsidiary or ancillary: *Cotman v Brougham* (*1918*). Even if there were such an independent objects clause it seems that an inherently subsidiary power to borrow cannot be converted into an independent object: *Re Introductions* (*1970*) ('a power to borrow cannot mean something in the air'). A clause similar to the one which permits the company to carry on any profitable business was upheld in *Bell Houses Ltd v City Wall Properties Ltd* (*1966*); thus the new activity might come within this clause and be *intra vires*, in which case the bank could sue to recover any loan made.

ANSWER A14

A company comes into existence when its certificate of incorporation is issued. Until the company is so incorporated no agent can make on its behalf a contract binding on the company when later incorporated. No agent can make a contract binding on his principal unless at the time when the contract is made the principal exists and has capacity to enter into the contract, nor can the company ratify the contract when it is incorporated: *Kelner v Baxter* (*1866*). Hence the company when incorporated could not hold Wharfe & Partners to the agreement on its behalf by Terry. There is no contract with the company enforceable by or against it.

In such a case as this however, *s. 9(2) ECA 1972* provides that the 'contract shall have effect as a contract entered into by the person [Terry] purporting to act for the company or as agent for it, and he shall be personally liable on the contract accordingly'. The partners could therefore hold Terry liable on the contract and although a promoter could not previously sue the other party on a contract made for a non-existent company, *s. 9* probably means that he can now do so. This seems to be the necessary result of the words 'have effects as a contract', i.e. it is a bilaterally binding agreement.

If so Terry could if he wishes hold the partners to the contract and assign his right to do so to the company when formed.

ANSWER A15

Two main arguments were adduced by the creditors who sought to get the debenture issued to Salomon set aside as invalid. Both arguments began from the undisputed fact that Salomon owned all the 20,007 issued shares though six shares were separately registered in the names of members of his family, i.e. they were his nominees.

In the High Court it was held that although the company was a separate person from Salomon it must on the facts be regarded as his nominee or agent. Salomon was therefore liable to the company's creditors and any assets to which he could lay prior claim under the debenture should be available to the creditors in satisfaction of Salomon's personal liability to them.

The Court of Appeal overruled the argument accepted in the High Court but reached the same conclusion by a different route. The Court of Appeal held that in laying down a minimum membership of seven (as it was at the time) the Companies Acts required 'Seven *independent* bona fide members'; one such member (Salomon) plus six nominees was not enough. The company had been unlawfully incorporated and Salomon must indemnify it against its liabilities.

The House of Lords overruled both arguments on the grounds that nothing in the Acts required members to hold shares in their own right and that on the facts the company was not the nominee or agent of Salomon. The company has acquired its business and assets by a valid purchase from Salomon and had given him valid security for the outstanding part of the purchase price. 'The company is at law a different person altogether from the subscribers to the memorandum' even though the formation of the company left the ultimate *control* of assets and the right to enjoy profits earned by those assets with Salomon (as sole owner) as before.

ANSWER A16

A company comes into existence on the date of issue of its certificate of incorporation. Until that date it does not exist and cannot enter into a contract binding on the company nor allot and issue shares. Accordingly if the meeting is held on 2 Jan. as proposed by Smith and Brown the transactions proposed will have no legal effect as regards the company. The subsequent issue of the certificate of incorporation has no retrospective effect to a period before the date of the certificate.

If Smith and Brown sign the contract for the purchase of the business on 2 Jan. they would become personally liable on the contract whether they signed as agents of the non-existent company or purported to make the company itself a party to the contract: *s. 9(2) ECA 1972. S. 9(2)* provides that it is to 'have effect as contract' with the implication that it is to be binding on both parties. Jones can certainly sue Smith and Brown for damages if the purchase is not completed by them for breach of implied warranty of authority.

The position over the allotment of shares by directors of a non-existent company is more obscure. The company has certainly not issued the shares: it cannot do so. The directors have received the subscription money, mainly from Evans and also from themselves, on the basis that shares are to be allotted. Any letters of allotment issued to allottees on 2 Jan. would be void.

If the directors repeat the procedure of allotting shares after incorporation of the company this would be a new transaction and would regularise the position. Otherwise the money must be returned. The directors can hardly be personally liable to perform the contract since it is not in their power as individuals to allot and issue shares. But they would be liable in damages if the company after incorporation failed to allot the shares. The directors should be advised of the liabilities which they would incur if they proceed as proposed. The best solution, if Jones will agree, is perhaps to sign a contract on 2 Jan. which expressly states that Smith and Brown can terminate it without liability to themselves if the company does not within a specified period enter into a new contract with Jones to replace the earlier contract. There is nothing which they can do to bind Evans to apply for shares when the company is formed. They must hope that at that later stage he will still be willing to do so.

ANSWER A17

CA 1980 introduces pre-exemption rights—directors when issuing new shares must offer them first to the existing shareholders in proportion to their holdings (*s. 17 CA 1980*), but the company may by special resolution resolve that these pre-exemption rights shall not apply. A and B could pass the necessary resolution. Moreover, directors must have the authority of the company either by resolution in general meeting or in the articles to allot relevant securities. This should present no problem in this case as the directors are the shareholders and C has insufficient votes to alter the articles or pass a resolution.

However, X requires that the objects and the articles shall first be altered. In each case a special resolution is required (*ss. 5 and 10 CA 1948*). A and B have between them 80% of the issued shares so they can carry a special resolution by a three quarter majority even if C casts his 20% of the votes against.

Under *s. 5*, C as holder of more than 15% of the issued shares can within 21 days appeal to the court against the resolution to alter the objects. Although the new main object is a complete departure from the 'business of general merchants' the court will probably treat this as an instance of 'advantageously combining' a new business with the original main object and so within the power of amendment given by *s. 5(1)(d)*: *Re Parent Tyre Co (1923)*. C is likely to fail in his application since there is no reason why the court should uphold his objection to a new main object which all three—A, B and C—contemplated when they bought the company.

The only ground on which C can object to the change in the articles is that the other three shareholders (A, B and X) will then have an entrenched right to be directors but he, as holder of only 500 shares, will not. However, if the change is in the interest of the company as a whole it is immaterial that some member thereby loses or fails to retain an advantage: *Shuttleworth v Cox Bros & Co (Maidenhead) Ltd (1927)*. However, the case of *Clemens v Clemens Bros Ltd (1976)* indicates that the court will sometimes intervene where a member is to be deprived of existing rights: but on the facts given it is difficult to identify any existing right which C is to lose. Similarly, it seems unlikely that *s. 75 CA 1980* (the 'unfairly prejudicial conduct' section) would help C.

ANSWER A18

A company is a separate legal entity distinct from its members and directors. The division between a company and its members, established in *Salomon's Case*, is called 'the veil of incorporation'. One consequence of the principle is that usually members of a limited company have no liability for its debts, if it become insolvent, beyond the amount due on their shares or (if it is a guarantee company) on their guarantees. A second consequence is that a company's assets are its property and are not treated as property of its members even though they own the company itself.

There are a number of exceptions to the rule and its application as stated above. Four exceptions can be found from the following:

(a) *Reduction of number of members below the legal minimum: s. 31 CA 1948*

Where the number of members is reduced below the statutory minimum (i.e. two) and the company carries on business while so reduced for six months, then all the members cognisant of the fact are severally liable for debts incurred after the six months.

(b) *Fraudulent trading: s. 332 CA 1948*

If, in the course of winding up, it appears that any business has been carried on with intent to defraud creditors, or for any fraudulent purpose, the court, on the application of the Official Receiver, liquidator, a creditor or a member, may declare that any persons who were knowingly parties to the fraud shall be personally liable without any limitations for all or any of the debts or other liabilities of the company. If a member of the company or even an outsider was implicated in the fraud he could be liable for the company's debts under this section.

(c) *Misdescription of company: s. 108 CA 1948*

Where agents sign as authorised signatories of the company any bill of exchange, promissory note, cheque or order for goods or money, and the name of the company is not mentioned thereon in legible characters, they incur personal liability. The name must be the corporate name (*Maxform SPA v B Mariani & Goodville Ltd* (*1979*)) and not just a trade name, and must include the word 'limited' if it is a private company and the words 'public limited company' if it is a public company.

(d) *Groups of companies: s. 154 CA 1948*

Where such a relationship exists, there are extensive rules regarding accounts and publicity, in which their separate legal entity is bypassed and the assets of subsidiaries are treated as if owned by the holding company.

(e) *Tax*

The residence of a company for purposes of liability to UK tax is determined by the test of 'central control and management', i.e. where its directors meet to determine questions of policy and management.

(f) *Fraud*

If a controlling shareholder uses the company as a separate person to carry out transactions which the shareholder himself is legally prevented from undertaking the company may be restrained by court order since the 'veil of incorporation' will be lifted to prevent its use as a means of dishonest evasion: *Gilford Motor Co Ltd v Horne* (*1933*).

Tutorial note

The civil aspect of *s. 332 CA 1948* described in this answer (fraudulent trading) applies only when the company goes into liquidation. Since *CA 1981* the criminal offence which is at the same time committed can be prosecuted even if the company is not wound up.

ANSWER A19

Where a company enters into a transaction *ultra vires* its objects, the transaction is void and of no effect. The other party to the transaction may however rely on *s. 9(1) ECA 1972* to enforce the contract. Tom has apparently acted in good faith but he cannot rely on *s. 9(1) ECA 1972* unless he can show that the transaction was also *decided on by the directors*. As there were previous purchases which were paid for by the company it may be that the directors had approved a continuing system of purchases from Tom. Otherwise an order placed by a single director on his own authority is outside *s. 9(1)*. Tom could not sue Harry personally in contract for the supply of goods as Harry indicates by the words 'Director for and on behalf of X Ltd' that he is only acting in the capacity of agent of the company and not personally. Tom could however sue Harry for breach of an implied warranty of authority—i.e. Harry guaranteed that he has the authority to enter into the particular transaction.

If Tom loses on the *ultra vires* point it is immaterial whether or not Harry had authority for the order; a director can never be authorised to make an *ultra vires* contract. But if the contract was *intra vires* the company in this case, Tom can probably establish that Harry has authority to commit the company to it. Articles in the form of *Table A* permit the delegation of authority by the board; Tom would not be entitled to assume that there had been a proper delegation under the rule in *Turquand's Case* but he could argue that by paying for the previous purchases the company had 'held out' Harry as an agent authorised to make such purchases: *Freeman and Lockyer Ltd v Buckhurst Park Properties Ltd* (*1964*). It is immaterial that Tom had not looked at the articles to see whether they are permitted such delegations.

ANSWER A20

In developing the proposition cited in the question Professor Gower lists as related advantages (1) limited liability, (2) separate ownership of property by the company (3) procedure for suing and being sued, (4) perpetual succession, (5) transferable shares, and (6) facilities for borrowing. Some of these advantages accrue to the company, for example borrowing with a floating charge as security, and indirectly to members, but others, such as limited liability or transferable shares, are advantages enjoyed mainly by the members. The question does not stipulate from whose standpoint the advantages are to be judged. As a matter of opinion limited liability and transferability of shares will be taken as outstanding advantages. By conferring on members favourable opportunities of investment they have promoted the development of companies as the main organized form of large scale business enterprise.

(1) *Limited liability*

The advantages of limited liability to members (provided of course that the company has been formed with limited liability and not, as it can be, as an unlimited company) are that the public can invest their money profitably in a business (separately owned by a company) without assuming personal liability for its losses (if any) in excess of the amount which they agree to contribute for their shares (or as guarantors if it is a company limited by guarantee). In this way the company on its side can attract investment support from a much wider circle than would be possible if the investors were sleeping partners in a partnership or even protected by the uncertain status of limited partners under the *Limited Partnership Act 1907* (which has the additional disadvantage that a limited partner may not take an active part in the management of the business).

The dependence of limited liability on the distinction between a company and its members was demonstrated by the decision (of the House of Lords) in *Salomon v Salomon & Co Ltd* (*1897*) which drew a sharp and clear line of division between the artificial corporate entity and its membership. It is because a company is a separate person with its own separate debts that its members can by the terms of their participation in it be excluded in all normal circumstances from liability beyond the amount payable or already paid in respect of their shares or guarantee as the case may be.

(2) *Transferability of shares*

In a company, unlike a partnership, the individual proprietors have no general relationship with each other (except such as the memorandum or articles of association may effect under *s. 20 CA 1948*). Each member has a stake in the company, measured and expressed in terms of his shareholding, as financial and other benefits (for example rights to dividend, return of capital and voting) and liability to pay what is due on the shares: *Borland's Trustee v Steel Bros & Co Ltd* (*1901*). As a result of this bilateral, but separate relationship between the company and each of its members, each member has rights of property which by their nature are (subject always to the articles of association) transferable without direct alteration of the similar rights of other members. Because shares are transferable they are in a technical and commercial sense marketable securities and as such an attractive and realisable investment.

This advantage of transferable shares is inherently a consequence of the distinction between a company and its members. By contrast, in a partnership the interest of each member is assignable but he cannot (without the consent of the other partners) admit the assignee to partner status as his successor in title.

The articles of association can, of course, restrict the right to transfer shares and some such restriction is common in a private company.

ANSWER A21

(a) Every company must have a registered office: *s. 23(1) CA 1976*. The situation of the office fixes the company's domicile and nationality but not its residence e.g. for tax purposes. Its memorandum must state the country in which the registered office is to be situate but not the actual address. A company registered under *CA 1948* may choose to be situate in England, Wales or Scotland. When the company is formed the documents delivered to the Registrar for that purpose include the intended address of the registered office and notice of any change of address must be given to the Registrar within 14 days of the change. The Registrar gives notice in the *London Gazette* of receipt of any notice of change of address: *s. 9(3) ECA 1972*.

The registered office is important in two respects. First, to serve a document on a company, such as a legal notice or a writ or summons issued by the court, it is sufficient to leave it or to send it by post to the registered office. Secondly, a company is required to maintain a number of registers, such as its registers of members, of directors and secretary, of directors' interests in its shares, of its charges (if any) and to make these registers available for inspection by the public or in some cases (such as the minutes of general meetings and the directors' service agreements) only by members or in other cases by members and creditors. All these registers and other prescribed documents must be kept at the registered office (or in some cases at an alternative place in the same country as the registered office of which notice must then be given to the Registrar).

The address of the registered office may be changed at any time. It is usually a matter within the directors' delegate powers of management but the company's articles may require a resolution of the members. As stated, notice of any change must be given to the Registrar within 14 days.

The registered office must always be at an address within the country specified for that purpose in the memorandum, i.e. England, Wales or

Scotland. A company may specify that its registered office shall only be in Wales. It is then entitled to use the Welsh language on its documents for certain purposes: *s. 30 CA 1976*. There is now no provision for the alteration of the situation clause, and thus it is presumed to be unalterable.

(b) A company is required to show on its letters and bills the name of the company (which must include the word 'limited' if it is a private company and the words 'public limited company' if it is public, or the appropriate abbreviations, 'Ltd' or 'Plc'), its number at the Companies Registry, the address of its registered office (identified as such), the place (i.e. country) of incorporation and if it is a limited company which may omit the word 'limited' from its name under *s. 25 CA 1981* or if it uses the Welsh equivalent, the fact that it is a limited company: *s. 9(7) ECA 1972*. Under *s. 201 CA 1948* it was necessary to give names or former names of its directors on its letters unless the Department of Trade had given it exemption and the nationality of its directors unless they were nationals of any of the member states of the European Community. This is now no longer necessary: *Sch. 3 para 11 CA 1981*; but if any director's name is given except in the text or as a signatory, the names of all directors, including any 'shadow' director, must be given.

If it is an investment company (*Part III CA 1980*) a company must describe itself as such.

Where a company is being wound up, whether compulsorily or voluntarily, or a receiver or manager has been appointed, all invoices, letters, bills etc. must contain a statement to that effect: *s. 338* and *s. 370 CA 1948* respectively.

ANSWER A22

(a) Under *CA 1980* a new public company is one that is limited by shares as a public company, includes a statement in its memorandum to this effect, and has a minimum authorised share capital of £50,000 (of which 25% must be allotted and paid up plus the whole of any premium before the company is entitled to commence business: *ss. 1 and 4 CA 1980*). A private company is any company which is not a public company.

If the company is to be limited by shares the liability of its shareholders is limited to the issued share capital plus any premium payable.

(b) (Any three of the following would suffice):

(i) The main difference is that a public company may offer its shares or debentures to the public whereas a private company may not as it is an offence to do so: *s. 15 CA 1980*.

(ii) A public company must have the statutory minimum authorised share capital—i.e. £50,000—and cannot trade or borrow until the Registrar issues a 'section 4 certificate' which will not be done until at least £50,000 in nominal value has been allotted of which at least 25% is paid up plus the whole of any premium. Any contracts made in contravention of this provision are valid and binding but the directors are jointly and severally liable with the company if it fails to perform its obligations. A private company need only have issued two shares (i.e. one per subscriber to the memorandum) and they can have a nominal value as low as ½p each. A private company can trade or borrow as soon as its certificate of incorporation has been issued.

(iii) A public company can issue shares for non-cash consideration but an independent expert's report is required on the value of the consideration: *s. 24 CA 1980*. Moreover, a public company cannot accept services as consideration for its shares: *s. 20(2) CA 1980*. These rules do not affect private companies.

(iv) A public company must issue a prospectus if it offers its shares or debentures to the public. A private company is not subject to the prospectus rules.

(v) A public company requires two directors, a private company need only have one.

These are not exhaustive but are prominent examples of the differences.

(c) The legal requirements to convert a private company into a public one are onerous compared with the pre-1980 situation where a private company merely altered its articles to delete certain restrictive clauses.

Conversion now requires:

(i) special resolution passed by the company authorising re-registration;

(ii) application in a specified form signed by a director or secretary delivered to the Registrar;

(iii) various other documents must be delivered to the Registrar, among them being copies of the altered memorandum and articles, a copy of a statement by the auditors, and a copy of the relevant balance sheet;

(iv) compliance with the minimum share capital requirements: *s. 5 CA 1980*.

ANSWER A23

It is the duty of the directors to ensure that the company's trading activities are *intra vires*, i.e. within the scope of its objects clause and matters incidental thereto.

The operation of taxi cabs would be within paragraph (1) of the existing objects because this includes all types of vehicles. But the use of the premises as a retail motor garage and the business of buying, selling and repairing cars are outside the scope of all three main objects.

The directors could be restrained by court injunction at the instance of the opposing minority and would be liable for breach of duty if they commit the company to *ultra vires* activities. They could also be personally liable to an outsider for breach of warranty of authority. But they can avoid this risk by procuring a suitable alteration of the objects under *s. 5 CA 1948*. Such alteration may be effected, among other purposes, to carry on some other business which under existing circumstances may conveniently or advantageously be combined with the existing business of the company. The directors' proposals fall within that wide description.

The directors should therefore convene a general meeting to consider and pass a special resolution to make suitable amendments to the objects clause. The opposing minority will presumably be unable to prevent the resolution being passed by the required 75% majority of votes cast. But if they hold at least 15% of the voting shares (or any class of them) they may within 21 days apply to the court which will consider their objections and will then either confirm the alterations (wholly or in part and with or without conditions) or reject them (or since *CA 1980* order the buying out of the objectors' shares).

If the alteration takes effect because no application is made to the court or any application is unsuccessful, a copy of the memorandum of association containing the altered objects clause must be filed at the Companies Registry within 15 days of the passing of the resolution or if application is made to the court within 15 days of the court confirming the alteration.

ANSWER A24

A pre-incorporation contract made on behalf of an as yet non-existent company by its promoters will make them personally liable for breach of warranty or authority: *Kelner v Baxter* (*1866*). The same case makes it clear that the company, when it is formed, cannot ratify the contract and relieve the promoters of their personal liability. A further problem for promoters is that, according to *Newborne v Sensolid* (*Great Britain*) *Ltd* (*1954*), while personally liable, such a promoter cannot sue if the other party to the contract defaults. However, *s. 9(2) ECA 1972*, while it confirms personal liability as in *Kelner v Baxter* probably negates *Newborne v Sensolid.* The weight of academic opinion is that such a promoter could now sue if the other party should default.

James and John should be advised of the danger of personal liability if they contract for the company before it receives its certificate of incorporation. If they are unconcerned by the risk, but worried that they might not be able to sue Tom Zed, they could take the contract in their own names and, if necessary, sue personally rather than rely on *s. 9(2) ECA 1972*.

If the risk of personal liability is too great for them, they will either have to withdraw entirely, or find another method to avoid liability. Possibly, if they do not mind the extra expense, they may wish to purchase a ready-made company which can take the contract immediately. Alternatively, they may be able to persuade Tom to grant an option which they can assign to the company when it is formed; or to agree to a clause releasing them from personal liability as and when the company is formed and ready to take over. These contractual arrangements are however entirely dependent on agreement with Tom. If he refuses, the only possibilities are withdrawal, a ready-made company or the risk of personal liability.

ANSWER A25

The power to appoint and remove a director rests primarily with the shareholders in general meeting; indeed it is not possible to contract out of their power of removal by ordinary resolution: *s. 184 CA 1948*. The shareholders then usually delegate all powers of management to the directors: *Table A Article 80*. But it is usual to provide in the articles of association that the board may appoint one or more of their number to the office of managing director for such period and on such terms as they see fit, and subject to the terms of any agreement entered into in any particular case, may revoke such appointment: *Table A Article 107*.

If a managing director is appointed to hold office merely on the terms of the articles he cannot rely on *s. 20 CA 1948* to enable him to enforce those terms even if he is a member of the company. By *s. 20* there is deemed to be a contract between the company and its members for the enforcement of member's rights, and a right to act as managing director is not a member's right: *Eley v Positive Government Security Life Assurance Co Ltd* (*1876*). Thus a managing director's appointment may be revoked at any time and without notice, as the articles provide. In *Read v Astoria Garage* (*Streatham*) *Ltd* (*1952*) the articles provided that the appointment of a managing director should 'be subject to determination *ipso facto*' if the company in general meeting so resolved. Read, who had been appointed on those terms, was removed from office by the board and their decision was ratified in general meeting. His claim that he was entitled to reasonable notice failed since his appoointment was strictly on the terms of the articles which gave him no such right. Moreover, as a managing director must also be a director, his removal by the shareholders under *s. 184 CA 1948* as a director would automatically terminate his appointment as managing director.

However, although the articles do not form a contract, they are evidence of terms upon which the director is serving and can be used as the basis for an implied contract outside the articles: *Re New British Iron Co* (*1898*) ('*Beckwith's Case*').

Where however the managing director is appointed under the articles and the company makes a separate service agreement with him, the actions of the company, i.e. either the board or the shareholders in general meeting, in terminating his appointment before the agreement expires is a breach of the separate contract: *Shindler v Northern Raincoats Co Ltd* (*1960*). Similarly an alteration of articles by the company to facilitate his removal as a means of terminating his appointment will not justify a breach of any separate contract: *Southern Foundries* (*1926*) *Ltd v Shirlaw* (*1940*) (managing director could not obtain an injunction to restrain removal but could sue for damages for premature termination of his fixed-term contract).

Where the board on appointing a managing director under the articles also specifies that he is to hold office for a particular period even if it is an uncertain period (as in the facts of the question), this provision becomes part of the separate contract, breach of which will give rise to a remedy in damages. As Jim is removed before the expiry of the term of his appointment, he may claim damages for breach of contract. He should be advised accordingly.

The separate agreement prevails over the articles and is not subject to any overriding power of immediate termination. In *Nelson v James Nelson & Sons Ltd* (*1914*), from which the facts of the question are taken, it was said that the power to terminate in the articles 'only gives the directors power to take away that which they have given *provided* that they have not bound themselves to give it for any period of time'.

Tutorial note

The rule introduced by *s. 47 CA 1980* that a director may only be granted a service agreement exceeding 5 years with the consent of the general meeting applies only to new service agreements entered into on or after 22 Dec. 1980.

ANSWER A26

Designation

Both public and private limited companies were required to include as the last word of their name, the word 'limited' (*s. 2*(*1*)(*a*) *CA 1948*) unless dispensation with this requirement was granted under *s. 19 CA 1948* (i.e. power to dispense with 'limited' in the name of charitable and other companies by the Department of Trade). *S. 2*(*1*) was intended to give publicity to the creditors of the fact that the shareholders' liability to contribute to the company's assets was limited to the amount they had agreed to subscribe for their shares. A creditor did not know from the name whether the company was a public or private one. Moreover, although the creditor knew that the company's liability was limited he did not know how much share capital has been issued—i.e. he did not know the extent to which it was limited. This follows from the fact that English Company Law did not insist on a minimum allotted share capital; it now does so insist but only for public companies. The new designation, 'public limited company' ('Plc' or Welsh equivalent if a Welsh company) for a public company means that a creditor knows from the company's name that it is public and has the 'guarantee' of a minimum share capital.

Private companies keep their pre-1980 designation—i.e. 'limited' (or 'Ltd.').

S. 19 CA 1948 now only applies to private companies; thus a public company *must* always use its designation, 'public limited company'.

Classification

A private company was defined in *s. 28 CA 1948* as a company which included in its articles, three restrictions—on the number of members (50), on the transfer of shares and on offering shares or debentures to the public. Any company which did not include these restrictions was automatically a public company. Moreover, a private company which did offer its shares or debentures to the public was treated for the purposes of the prospectus rules as a public company. *CA 1980* defines a public company as a company limited by shares which states in its memorandum that it is a public company and is registered or re-registered as such, which involves in particular capital of at least the authorised minimum, i.e. £50,000.

A private company is any company that is not a public company. *S. 28 CA 1948* has been repealed but it has become a criminal offence for a private company to offer its shares to the public: *s. 15 CA 1980.*

Once a private company has received its certificate of incorporation, it may commence business in its own right. A public company, however, cannot trade or borrow money until additional requirements in relation to the share capital have been complied with—viz. £50,000 share capital has been allotted with at least 25% of the nominal value paid up and all of any premium: *s. 4 CA 1980.* The old trading certificate, *s. 109 CA 1948*, has been abolished. On compliance with *s. 4 CA 1980*, the Registrar shall issue a certificate of compliance and the company will have the right to commence business. If contracts are made before the issue of the 'section 4 certificate' they are valid and binding but the directors will be jointly and severally liable with the company if it defaults.

ANSWER A27

Jerry and Tom are clearly seeking one of the main advantages of a limited company, namely limited liability. They therefore need a private limited company as at this stage they are not likely to be seeking investment from the public. They will be the only directors and shareholders and the company will therefore depend upon mutual trust between them and be what the courts have come to call a 'quasi-partnership company': *Ebrahimi v Westbourne Galleries Ltd* (*1973*).

The company will be able to trade or borrow immediately its certificate of incorporation is issued, so there will be no added complication of obtaining a 'section 4 certificate' (*s. 4 CA 1980*) as in the case of a Plc.

Approval of the proposed name by the Registrar of Companies is no longer required since 26 Feb. 1982, nor will the consent of the Secretary of State or any other body be needed under *CA 1981 Part II*, as the proposed name is not one which is prohibited or restricted by the Act. However, it is wise, before incorporating the company, to search the index of names kept by the Registrar. He can order the change of a name which is the same as or too like an existing name within 12 months of the incorporation and obviously this would involve the new company in considerable unnecessary expense.

The professional advisers of Jerry and Tom will then secure registration of the new company by lodging with the Registrar:

(a) The memorandum of association subscribed by at least two subscribers (probably Jerry and Tom). The document must be witnessed and opposite the signatures the number of shares initially subscribed for (usually one each) will be shown. It is necessary to ensure that the objects clause in the memorandum is suitable so that *ultra vires* problems are unlikely. Clearly, the authorised capital will need to be at least £30,000.

(b) The articles of association signed and witnessed by the same people. Unless Jerry and Tom have special requirements, *Table A* will be adopted with conventional amendments.

(c) The statement of first directors and secretary (incorporating their signed consents) and signed by the subscribers.

(d) A statement of the address of the registered office.

(e) A declaration of compliance with the requirements of the Companies Acts in respect of formation, signed by the director engaged in the formation or any of the first directors or secretary.

(f) A statement of capital on formation, on which capital duty will have to be paid at £1 per £100 (i.e. a total of £1 if only two shares are initially subscribed for).

(g) A fee (at present £50).

The Registrar will shortly issue the certificate of incorporation, which is conclusive as to the proper compliance with registration formalities. A board meeting will be needed for formal approval of the necessary contract for sale of the business to the company, ideally entirely in exchange for shares to be issued equally to Jerry and Tom (there are capital gains tax advantages in ensuring that the consideration consists entirely of shares); and a return of allotments and a copy of the contract will need to be delivered to the Registrar within one month: *s. CA 1948*. *Ad valorem* capital duty will be payable on the allotment and stamp duty on any conveyance or transfer of the assets to the company. The company's minute book will need to be written up and particulars of the allotment shown in the Register of members.

ANSWER A28

(a) *S. 13 CA 1948* provides for the issue by the Registrar of Companies of a Certificate of Incorporation. The life of the company commences when the certificate is issued and the certificate is conclusive evidence that the registration formalities have been complied with.

'Incorporation' implies that the company is a body corporate ('corporation') which is a separate legal entity, an artificial or 'juristic' person with a life of its own entirely separate and distinct from its members. Even a so-called 'one man company' in which one person owns substantially all the shares (except for a share or a few shares held by a nominee) is a separate legal entity and can owe money to its shareholders: *Salomon v Salomon & Co Ltd* (*1897*).

A company has a common seal and enjoys perpetual succession, the right to own property and can sue and be sued in its own name.

A limited company's members may have the benefit of limited liability in the following ways:

(i) If the company is limited by shares, the liability of the members to contribute to the company's debts is limited to the nominal value of the shares held by them, plus any share premium.
(ii) A guarantee company's memorandum sets out a predetermined form which each member guarantees to pay, if need be, on liquidation. Each member's liability is limited to that sum.

It is possible (but unusual) for a company to be limited both by shares and by guarantees but no further companies of this dual nature are possible since *CA 1981*. 'Limited Company' is something of a misnomer, because it is not the liability of the company which is limited, but the liability of the members for its debts.

(b) There are numerous case-law and statutory examples of 'lifting the veil of incorporation'. The two examples required to be given could be selected from, among others, the following:

Examples under CA 1948

(i) Reduction of number of members below legal minimum. *S. 31* provides that where the company has carried on business with less than the prescribed number of members (now two for any company, public or private: *s. 2(1) CA 1980*) for more than six months, every person who is a member during the time when the company so carries on business after those six months have passed shall, if he is aware of the irregularity, be personally liable for all the company's debts contracted during that time.
(ii) Bills of exchange signed on behalf of the company without mentioning, or without correctly mentioning, the company's name. *S. 108(4)* makes an officer who signs such a bill personally liable on it unless it is honoured by the company. *Parrish v British Airways (1979)* is an example of personal liability arising where a cheque named the company incorrectly ('Limited' was omitted).
(iii) Fraudulent trading. In the event of winding up, *s. 332(1)* of the Act allows the court to declare that any persons who were knowingly parties to carrying on the business with intent to defraud creditors or for other fraudulent purpose shall be personally responsible for all or any of the company's debts without any limitation of liability.
(iv) Department of Trade inpectors investigating a company's affairs may also investigate the affairs of any subsidiary or holding company (*s. 166*).
(v) Group accounts. Where a company has subsidiaries, there is an obligation (with exceptions) to lay group accounts before the holding company (*s. 150*).

Case law examples

The courts will 'lift the veil' to determine:
(i) whether a company is an 'enemy' in wartime, for the purpose of applying prohibitions against trading with the enemy: *Daimler Co Ltd v Continental Tyre and Rubber Co (Great Britain) Ltd (1916)*;

(ii) whether a company is a mere sham, formed in order to circumvent a legal obligation. *Gilford Motor Co Ltd v Horne* (*1933*) is an example of this—the company was held to be a device formed to allow its principal shareholder to evade a covenant that he would not solicit customers from his former employer. A further example (an unsuccessful attempt to evade specific performance of a contract for the sale of land) is *Jones v Lipman* (*1962*);
(iii) in the case of a quasi-partnership company (i.e. a small private company run like a partnership) the court will recognise the similarity to a partnership and so 'lift the veil' to permit winding up on the just and equitable ground (*s. 222*(*f*) *CA 1948*) by a director/shareholder who is excluded from management: *Ebrahimi v Westbourne Galleries Ltd* (*1973*).

ANSWER A29

(a) The common law rule about pre-incorporation contracts is that they are not binding on the company as before incorporation it lacks a personality and so has no contractual (or any other) capacity. Where the persons contracting on the non-existent company's behalf purported to make a binding contract (and not just a provisional agreement which could be adopted consequently after incorporation) there was at common law likely to be a presumption that those persons must have intended liability. This was particularly strong when the contract had been executed by the other party on the assumption that there must be a binding obligation on somebody: *Kelner v Baxter* (*1866*). At common law there was a further possibility that the company only had made the contract, and that the human intermediary was simply authenticating the company's contract and was contracting neither as agent nor as principal: *Newborne v Sensolid* (*Great Britain*) *Ltd* (*1954*).

In that case, the plaintiff was not permitted to sue suppliers for non-delivery of goods he ordered on behalf of a company before its incorporation.

S. 9(*2*) *ECA 1972* now gives a strong presumption against the *Newborne v Sensolid* situation. It provides that where a contract purports to be made by a company, or by a person as agent for a company, at a time when the company has not been formed, then subject to any agreement to the contrary the contract shall have effect as a contract entered into by the person purporting to act for the company or as agent for it, and he shall be personally liable.

Whereas, therefore, the Act confirms *Kelner v Baxter* (promoter who ordered wine for non-existent company held personally liable on the basis of breach of warranty of authority) it probably destroys *Newborne v Sensolid* so that such a promoter can now sue.

(b) The company cannot, upon incorporation, ratify a pre-incorporation contract even if its 'agent' purported to act on its behalf. Ratification operates retrospectively and is not available if there was no principal in existence at the time of the transaction: *Natal Land Co Ltd v Pauline*

Colliery Syndicate Ltd (*Privy Council 1904*). Application for order of specific performance of a pre-incorporation contract was refused; the Privy Council advised that even if the agent could be treated as contracting on behalf of the unincorporated company or on behalf of the company when incorporated, it was clear that the company could not by ratification obtain the benefit of a pre-incorporation contract. After incorporation, a new contract could be made on the same terms as the old.

The difficulty from the promoter's point of view is that the company cannot relieve him of personal liability without the consent of the other party. The Jenkins Committee recommended that companies should be allowed unilaterally to adopt a pre-incorporation contract, and that pending such adoption the individuals purporting to act on the company's behalf should be personally liable. That recommendation has not been enacted.

(c) In *Ashbury Railway Carriage & Iron Co Ltd v Riche* (*1875*) the House of Lords concluded that a contract beyond the objects in a company's memorandum of association was void from the beginning and could not be ratified even if all the shareholders approved. To allow ratification would be to allow the directors to do that which the company itself could not, and then permit the shareholders to authorise, by ratification that which was *ultra vires*. This common law rule has not been changed by *s. 9 ECA 1972*.

A company may not take advantage of its own *ultra vires* transaction, even when the company has purported to ratify that transaction. *S. 9*(*1*) protects any third parties, not the company itself.

The issue here is quite distinct from that which arises when directors or agents exceed the authority which a company has given them, but still transact within the company's objects. Such a transaction could, and can, be ratified subject only to the general limits on ratification: it is *intra vires* the company and the company can adopt what it could have done itself.

ANSWER A30

(a) By *s. 5*(*1*) *CA 1948* a company may by special resolution alter its objects for any one of the following seven purposes: to carry on its business more economically, or more efficiently; to attain its main purpose by new or improved means; to enlarge or change the local area of its operations; to carry on some business which, under existing circumstances, may conveniently or advantageously be combined with the business of the company; to restrict or abandon any of its existing objects; to sell or dispose of the whole or any part of its undertaking; to amalgamate with any other company or body of persons.

(b) An application for cancellation of the alteration of a company's objects may be made by either:

(i) the holders of not less than 15% in nominal value of the issued capital or any class thereof (and if the company is not limited by shares by not less than 15% of its membership); or
(ii) the holders of not less than 15% of the company's debentures being those secured by a floating charge and issued prior to Dec. 1947.

No person who has consented to or voted in favour of the proposed alteration of the company's objects is entitled to make application for that alteration to be cancelled. The result of a successful application to cancel an alteration is that such alteration has no effect except insofar as it is approved by the Court.

The Court may refuse or confirm the alteration wholly or in part or impose conditions of approval, e.g. that the interests of dissentient members are purchased. Any application must be made within twenty-one days after the resolution altering the objects. If an application for cancellation is made, the company must notify the Registrar immediately, and within a prescribed time limit of the date of the Court's order cancelling or confirming the alteration deliver to the Registrar an office copy of the order and an amended memorandum (where appropriate).

If the company seeks to alter the objects clause for purposes outside those permitted by *s. 5*, even a single shareholder who cannot satisfy the 15% requirement may apply to the Court which must then cancel the alteration. Once 21 days have gone by, however, the company is safe from any such application.

(c) The above procedure for the alteration of a company's objects is unaffected by *s. 9 ECA 1972*. That provision enables an outsider who has acted in good faith in a transaction decided by the directors to enforce a contract against a company which has acted beyond its capacity as determined by its objects, but it does not enable the company which has acted *ultra vires* to enforce such a contract against the outsider. Thus, a company which intends to pursue a course of business beyond the scope of its objects must be properly advised to amend those objects prior to embarking on the new venture. The procedure for the alteration of objects is not retrospective in operation. Thus, unless *s. 5* is utilised prior to the company's involvement in a new venture, the company may find itself liable on a contract which it is itself unable to enforce.

Likewise directors who commit the company to an *ultra vires* transaction in which it uses money or property may be sued by the shareholders for breach of their common law duties of care and skill; alternatively, if it is the outsider who suffers loss (in a case where he is unprotected by *s 9 ECA 1972*) he may sue the directors concerned for breach of warranty of authority, or if they deliberately lied, in the tort of deceit.

ANSWER A31

(a) *Rights against the company.* The section quoted (*s. 20 CA 1948*) binds the company and the members to each other in accordance with the terms of the memorandum and the articles. The members are bound in their capacity as members, and cannot claim benefits or incur liabilities under the memorandum or articles in any other capacity.

Examples:

In *Hickman v Kent or Romney Marsh Sheep Breeders' Association* (*1915*) the articles provided that disputes between the association and any members should be referred to arbitration. Hickman, a member, brought an action against the association. It was granted a stay of proceedings on the ground that the articles obliged Hickman to submit the dispute to arbitration.

In *Wood v Odessa Waterworks Co* (*1889*) the articles empowered the directors to declare a dividend. The company resolved to issue debenture bonds in place of a dividend. The court, interpreting the articles as requiring any dividend to be paid in cash, held that the proposed issue was a breach of the articles and granted Wood an injunction restraining the company from implementing the resolution.

In *Pender v Lushington* (*1887*) it was held that in the event of a company refusing to count a member's properly exercised votes, the company could be compelled to do so because of the contractual nature of the provision in the articles to that effect.

(b) *Disputes between members*. The section allows members to enforce their rights against each other, in their capacity as members.

Examples:

In *Rayfield v Hands* (*1960*) the dispute related to a clause in the articles which required the directors to take, equally between them at a fair valuation, the shares of any member who wished to transfer shares. Rayfield, a member, sought to enforce this provision against the directors. Vaisey J concluded that the relationship in issue was one between members, and on this and other grounds declared that the directors were bound to take the shares equally between them. The decision would have been otherwise if the directors had not themselves been members (and it should be noted that directors are not obliged to be members unless, in a particular company, there is a requirement that they shall hold qualification shares).

In *Beattie v E & F Beattie Ltd* (*1938*) the articles contained a clause that disputes between members, or between the company and a member, should be referred to arbitration. Beattie brought a representative action on behalf of herself and the other members claiming that the company had improperly paid fees to one of its directors (who was joined as defendant). The director sought a stay of proceedings on the basis of the arbitration clause. The Court of Appeal concluded that the issue was between the company and the director in his capacity as a director. The contractual force given to the articles by the Act was limited to matters which applied to members in their capacity as members. The stay of proceedings was accordingly refused.

(c) *Rights on non-members named in the articles*. The articles as such cannot constitute a contract between the company and a third person.

Examples:

In *Eley v Positive Government Security Life Assurance Co Ltd* (*1876*), Eley was named in the articles as solicitor to the company, with right to transact all its legal business. Later the company placed legal business with other solicitors. Eley sued the company for breach of contract. The Court of Appeal concluded that the articles did not constitute a contract between Eley and the company.

A contract between the company and a third party may however *incorporate* provisions from the articles as contractual terms. These terms can be incorporated by implication. The basis on which the provisions are incorporated may imply a right in the company to modify the terms of that contract by altering its articles. This was so in *Re New British Iron Co* (*'Beckwith's Case'*) (*1898*) where it was held that if directors act without express contracts, the court may infer from their conduct a contract in the terms described in the articles. The court in these cases in effect used the articles as evidence to clarify the terms (e.g. amount of remuneration) of the quite separate contract with the company.

In (a), (b) and (c) above, it is clear that *s. 20* creates a contract only for *members* in connection with *membership matters*.

ANSWER B1

The directors should ensure that they have power under the articles of association to issue shares and before they exercise any power to allot such shares (relevant securities), they must be authorised to do so, either by the company in general meeting or the articles of the company. Any such authority granted to the directors cannot exceed five years unless renewed by the shareholders; moreover the authority granted can be revoked or varied at any time: *s. 14 CA 1980*. Any power to issue new shares must be exercised in good faith and for a proper purpose, i.e. to raise capital which the company needs and not for an extraneous purpose such as altering the balance of votes: *Bamford v Bamford* (1970). In an attempt to restrict the powers of directors to issue shares for such collateral purposes, *s. 17 CA 1980* provides that new securities ranking *pari passu* with existing ones must first be offered to the existing shareholders in proportion to their holdings at the same price or less than they are to be offered to others. This rule applies, effectively, only to equity shares and may be excluded by a private company expressly in its memorandum or articles or if those documents contain a provision inconsistent with the pre-emption requirements of *s. 17*. Also, a power to allot shares given under *s. 14* may be coupled with a power to do so without following the *s. 17* pre-emption requirements.

Although a director is obliged to obtain for the company the maximum practicable premium for its shares, it is not evidence of a breach of this duty if the director is offering them at a lower price to existing shareholders under a rights issue, as long as the shares are not issued at a discount.

If the directors, having complied with *s. 17 CA 1980*, still have shares to allot, they may only offer them to the public if they issue a prospectus (but as there are identical shares already in existence an abridged form of prospectus would suffice): *s. 38 CA 1948*. Any premium must be credited to a statutory share premium account and may thereafter only be used for a specified capital purpose, i.e. it may not be distributed as dividend: *s. 56 CA 1948*. A return of allotments must be made and 1% capital duty paid (on consideration received) within one month: *s. 52 CA 1948*.

ANSWER B2

The remedy of rescission of a contract to subscribe for shares resulting from an untrue prospectus is lost if the shareholder after discovering the true facts affirms the contract by exercising his rights as a shareholder. The actions described in (a), (b) and (c) have all been held to be the exercise of those rights resulting in loss of the right to rescind. As an alternative remedy A could sue the directors for compensation under *s. 43 CA 1948*. As the prospectus was 'fraudulent' the directors must have known that it was untrue (or been indifferent as to its truth) and so the statutory defences under *s. 43* would not be available (fraud implies knowledge: *Derry v Peek* (*1889*)). If however there is difficulty in establishing fraud, A might sue for damages for common law negligence (*Hedley Byrne v Heller* (*1964*)) or by statute (*Misrepresentation Act 1967*), but the benefit of using *s. 43* is that unless the defendants can establish one of the statutory defences (in effect show they had reasonable grounds for their statements) they will be liable to compensate the plaintiff for loss suffered by subscribing on the faith of the untrue statement. The onus of proof is on the defendants: the plaintiff does not, under *s. 43*, need to prove fraud or negligence—it is for the defendants to disprove it.

Anthony should be advised accordingly.

ANSWER B3

(a) When a shareholder wishes to transfer part only of his holding he may send the share certificate for his entire holding and the transfer form to the company which endorses the transfer 'certificate lodged' and returns it to him. The certificate is retained for cancellation when the transfer has been presented for registration. By certification the company represents to any person acting in good faith that a document has been lodged (and will be retained by the company) which shows that the transferor has *prima facie* title to the shares or debentures: *s. 79 CA 1948*.

(b) If a mistake is made in the certification, i.e. if no certificate has been lodged (or if it is returned to the transferor), the company is liable to any person who suffers loss in reliance on the certified transfer, e.g. because the transferor using his wrongly returned share certificate transfers the shares to another person who becomes the registered holder: *Longman v Bath Electric Tramways Ltd (1905)*. But the company has no liability to any other person, e.g. a transferee to whom the transferor might deliver another (uncertified) transfer with his share certificate. Only the person with the certificated transfer has a claim against the company. If he loses the shares because another transferee of the same shares gets registered first, the company must compensate him because it made the fraud possible by wrongly returning the share certificate to the seller.

ANSWER B4

S. 42 CA 1981 provides that it is unlawful for a company to give financial assistance (which includes a gift, loan, security indemnity, or guarantee) whether directly or indirectly to enable a person to acquire shares in the company or assist in the discharge of a liability incurred as a result of that acquisition.

The main test is—what was the purpose or main purpose of the transaction? If the purpose was to give financial assistance it is unlawful.

The facts are a simplified version of *Selangor United Rubber Estates Ltd v Cradock (1968)* where it was held that *s. 54 CA 1948* had been infringed. *S. 42* reformulates the rule laid down in *s. 54* in more precise terms and provides a number of exceptions, by which a company may provide assistance for the purchase of its shares. These include loans in the ordinary course of a company's business, loans to an employees' share scheme and loans which are an incidental part of some larger purpose of the company. From the facts given none of these exceptions would apply and *s. 42* has been infringed.

S. 42(12) provides that when a company gives unlawful financial assistance the company and any other officer involved in the transaction should be liable to a term of imprisonment not exceeding two years or a fine or both. Thus, both the company and the officers authorising the transaction would be guilty of a criminal offence.

Under *s. 54* it was also held that if a company gives unlawful financial assistance by way of guarantee of a loan or security for it, those commitments are invalid since they support an illegal transaction. The merchant bank would therefore lose its security as this rule is likely to be the same for security declared unlawful by *s. 42*.

The position may be different if Shops Plc were a private limited company and the requirements of *ss. 43 and 44 CA 1981* were satisfied. If they follow the strict procedure specified in the Act they will be able to finance the purchase of their own shares.

ANSWER B5

(a) Under mortgage law any condition of a loan which postpones the mortgagor's right to repay the loan on reasonable notice (usually six months) is void as clogging the equity of redemption.

(b) The words 'by reason only' in *s. 89 CA 1948* indicate that the rule referred to in (a) has no application to company borrowings which may be for an unlimited period but other rules of equity on clogging the equity are not affected: *Knightsbridge Estates Trust Ltd v Byrne* (*1940*). If, for example, the mortgage also provides that commercial advantages secured by the lender are to continue after the mortgage has been redeemed that clause would be invalid if, but only if, it was considered unreasonable. In *Kreglinger v New Patagonia Meat Co* (*1914*) a priority right to purchase the borrower's products for a minimum period of five years was upheld.

(c) An irredeemable debenture is one which has no fixed date for repayment. The loan continues until the company either defaults on the terms of the debenture or goes into liquidation. An irredeemable debenture does not therefore mean that the money will never be repaid.

ANSWER B6

As the receiver has been appointed under a floating charge created within the previous twelve months his appointment could become void if the company goes into liquidation within the next six months: *s. 322 CA 1948*. The receiver would then be liable to account for the assets within his control to the liquidator. The receiver should obtain an indemnity from the bank which appointed him against the risks of that eventuality. A receiver is not bound by the contracts of the company made before he was appointed but he should seek the leave of the court if he proposes to repudiate contracts in such a way as would injure the company's goodwill: *Re Newdigate Colliery Co* (*1912*) (where leave was refused in circumstances like those of the question). If the receiver makes contracts as receiver of the company, he is personally liable on them but has a right of indemnity against the company's assets: *s. 369(2) CA 1948*. That indemnity might not be sufficient if goods supplied are defective. He would be wise to require the bank also to indemnify him (if under the debenture he is made an agent of the company and not of the bank).

ANSWER B7

Failure to register in the company's register any charge over its assets created by the company renders its officers, if they knew of the omission, liable to a default fine of £1,000 maximum (increased from £50 by *CA 1980*) but it does not affect the validity of the charge. The receiver would be wise to check whether there has also been a failure to register the charges at the Companies Registry under *s. 95 CA 1948*. The latter omission would affect the validity of the charges if a liquidation ensued because they would then be void as against the liquidator and creditors and it would be too late to apply for court consent for late registration outside the 21 day limit imposed by *s. 95*. This would destroy the validity of the receiver's appointment. If not validly appointed he could be liable for unauthorised interference with the company's assets.

At the time of his appointment the six months' period (for fraudulent preference) under *s. 320 CA 1948* has expired and so the fixed charge could not be invalidated on that account. But the floating charge (which is the sole basis of the receiver's control of assets other than the premises) could become invalid if the company went into liquidation up to Jan. 1982, under *s. 322 CA 1948*.

ANSWER B8

(a) A may apply to the court under *s. 101 CA 1948* for an order for late registration on grounds of inadvertence etc. (which must be explained) in failing to register within the prescribed 21 days. The court would only permit late registration of A's charge on condition that, although created earlier, it should rank behind the charges in favour of B and C both of which took effect before A's charge could be registered late: *Watson v Duff Morgan and Vermont (Holdings) Ltd (1974)*. Even if late registration is sanctioned A might find his charge invalidated if the company goes into liquidation within 12 months of its creation: *s. 322 CA 1948*.

(b) C's fixed charge attached to the factory as soon as it was created. It is a breach of the terms of B's charge but B cannot rely on that (and will be postponed to C since B's charge had not crystallised when C's charge was created) unless B can prove that when C's charge was created C had actual knowledge of the restriction in B's charge. Mere disclosure of the restriction in the registered particulars of B's charge at the Companies Registry is not enough: *Wilson v Kelland (1910)*.

ANSWER B9

(a) Since the two classes of shares have the same rights (other than the preferential rights to dividends of the preference shares) the proposed uniform reduction of share capital is not of itself a variation of the rights of either class against the other (although—as appears in (b) below—it is *indirectly* prejudicial to the preference shareholders). The variation of rights procedure of the articles of association and *s. 72 CA 1948* therefore does not apply.

The procedure for the reduction is prescribed by *ss. 66–69 CA 1948*. There must be power in the articles of association to reduce share capital; if there is no such power the articles must first be amended by special resolution (*s. 10*) to create the power. The company then passes a special resolution to cancel 80p per share of the capital paid up on shares of both classes and applies to the court for approval of the reduction (*s. 67*). As the reduction does not affect the amount of the company's assets available for payment of its debts the court is not required to invite and consider objections by creditors. But it may do so if it sees fit. The court would also consider the objections (if any) of the preference shareholders. Since they have no priority in repayment of capital there is no reason why the court should not approve a reduction under which both classes of share are to be equally reduced. The reduction takes effect when the court order approving it is issued and filed at the Companies Registry (*s. 68*).

(b) The preference shareholders have reason to object to the reduction since their 6% dividend (payable on the amount paid up) will be reduced from 6p per £1 share pa to 1⅕p only (on a 20p share). The ordinary shares as equity are not so affected.

(c) The preference shareholders cannot object to the reduction as a variation of their class rights since their right to 6% on the amount paid up is not to be varied as a ratio. Its variation in amount reflects the preference shareholders' loss of capital (against which they have no safeguard—see (a) above). If they have no justification for objecting to their proportionate loss of paid up capital the consequence of that loss in terms of dividend must be accepted. The court will listen to their objection when the company applies under *s. 67* but is unlikely to uphold it (*Re Mackenzie & Co* (*1916*) where the same issue was considered).

Moreover the preference shareholders could not use their votes (3,000 out of a total of 15,000) to block the passing of the special resolution (under *s. 66*) for a uniform capital reduction, i.e. the ordinary shareholders have the required three quarters majority of votes.

ANSWER B10

(a) A receiver appointed in a debenture holders' action, i.e. appointed by the court, is personally liable at common law (*Moss Steamship Co Ltd v Whinney* (*1912*)) on any contracts which he makes for the company unless the contract otherwise provides. But he has a right of indemnity out of the company's assets subject to the debenture holders' charge. In modern practice a receiver endeavours to trade on strictly cash terms so that any liability on contracts made by him is immediately discharged out of the company's available cash; credit transactions are avoided. But this is a matter of practice not law; not all contractual obligations (e.g. claims for defective goods supplied by the company on the receiver's contracts), can be liquidated in this way. A receiver therefore often seeks an indemnity from the debenture holder as a condition of accepting the appointment.

(b) The appointment of a receiver by the court does not of itself usually affect contracts of the company outstanding at the time of the appointment. The one exception is that contracts of employment of the company's employees are automatically terminated. If the receiver continues to use their services he is deemed to re-employ them under new contracts: *Reid v Explosives Co* (*1887*).

The receiver may either perform the existing contracts or repudiate them. If he performs them they are still the company's contracts on which he has no personal liability. If breaking an existing contract will injure the company's goodwill the receiver must first obtain the sanction of the court before doing so. In reaching its decision the court will consider the long-term interests of the company as well as the immediate interests of the debenture holders whom the receiver represents. But the receiver will not be prohibited from breaking a contract if in performing it he will have to borrow (and assume personal liability for the loan).

(*c*) The appointment of a receiver by the court operates as a suspension of the directors' powers to deal with the property charged. Directors who are also employees of the company are affected as in (b)—i.e. *Reid's Case*; but they do not cease to be directors and their responsibilities as such continue.

ANSWER B11

(a) It is assumed that the directors have the requisite authority from the shareholders to make this issue (*s. 14 CA 1980*) and the issue is within the authorised share capital.

The issue of shares for a consideration other than cash, i.e. in this case in exchange for shares of B Ltd, is permissible but the return of allotments must have attached to it a copy or particulars of the contract of acquisition: *s. 52 CA 1948*. Consideration to support a contract must be sufficient—i.e. of some monetary value—but need not be adequate, and the parties to the contract are free to make their own bargain.

Where, as in *Head v Ropner Holdings* (*1952*), the net asset value of the company whose shares are acquired exceeds the nominal value of the shares issued (in this case by A Ltd) the excess should be treated as share premium subject to the restrictions of *s. 56 CA 1948*. Thus, a notional 25p per share should be placed in the share premium account. This case and *Shearer v Bercain* (*1980*) effectively outlawed 'merger accounting' whereby (under ED3) the creation of a share premium account could (it was thought) be ignored in certain types of merger. *CA 1981* therefore modifies the position and relaxes the rules on share premium accounts to make it unnecessary to 'lock' the excess of the true value of the assets of the acquired company into a share premium account where (*inter alia*) a 90% minimum holding is acquired. It is not possible to tell from the question whether there has been such a merger here.

(b) In this case the yardstick of net asset value suggests that A Ltd is not obtaining full consideration for its shares; if that is so it would on these facts be issuing its shares at a discount on their nominal value which is not permitted: *Ooregum Mining Co v Roper* (*1892*) and now *s. 21 CA 1980*. *S. 57 CA 1948* which provided a limited exception to this principle has now been repealed, but in any case would not have applied as the *s. 57* procedure was only available to companies incorporated for at least one year.

However, asset value is merely one indication of the value to be put on shares of B Ltd. The merger of A and B may offer prospects of greater profitability for both companies. If the directors consider that the shares of B Ltd are worth an amount at least equal to the nominal value of the shares of A Ltd to be issued in exchange and enter the shares of B Ltd in their books at that value, their judgement, unless it is obviously not made in good faith and for sufficient reason, is unlikely to be set aside: *Re Wragg* (*1897*). In that case there is no issue of shares of A Ltd at a discount; there is an acquisition of assets (shares of B Ltd) at a possible over-value, which may be evidence of a breach of directors' duty—i.e. the duty to act in the best interest of the company.

If the company were a public company, on issuing the shares for a consideration other than cash it must obtain an independent valuation of the prosposed consideration: *s. 24 CA 1980*, but this provision is dispensed with if the shares are issued in connection with a merger, which might be the case in the problem.

ANSWER B12

(a) The prospectus rules apply not only to a direct offer to the public of shares or debentures made by the company itself but also to a re-sale to the public of shares from a block allotment previously made to an issuing house (usually a merchant bank). *S. 45 CA 1948* provides that a prospectus includes an offer on re-sale if either the offer is made within six months of the previous allotment by the company to the issuing house or if the company has not at the time of the offer on re-sale been paid the consideration on the shares or debentures, i.e. if it is to be paid out of money to be received from the public. A prospectus issued as an offer for sale must comply with all the general prospectus rules and also state the net amount to be received by the company from the issuing house and where the contract or allotment to the issuing house may be inspected. At least two directors, or if the issuing house is a firm at least half the partners, must join with the directors of the company in signing the copy of the prospectus to be filed at the Companies Registry.

(b) A prospectus must include a report by the auditors (or in certain cases other reporting accountants) on the profits, losses and dividends of the company and its subsidiaries (and of any business or company to be acquired out of the proceeds of the issue) for five years and a statement of assets and liabilities at the latest accounting date. In preparing these consolidated figures some adjustment of figures taken from audited accounts of individual companies may well be necessary. The prospectus itself must indicate what adjustments have been made (*Sch. 4 para. 29*), and a statement of adjustments signed by the auditors or other reporting accountants giving their reasons must be attached to the signed copy of the prospectus filed at the Companies Registry: *s. 41 CA 1948*.

(c) To ensure that all the shares or debentures offered by the prospectus are taken up it is standard practice to arrange that the issue is underwritten, i.e. the underwriters agree to subscribe for all shares or debentures for which the public may not apply. For that service the company pays to the underwriters a commission which may not exceed 10% of the issue price (it is usually very much less): *s. 53 CA 1948*. The amount of the commission must be disclosed in the prospectus. Underwriters may also agree to subscribe unconditionally and may be paid a commission for doing so but not as a means of evading the rule against issue of shares at a discount.

ANSWER B13

A trustee for debenture holders is appointed for the purpose of protecting their interests, i.e. he is their representative in dealing with the company, takes the necessary steps to enforce their rights, receives information from the company and, if he sees fit, gives consent on their behalf to the company where that consent is necessary. He may of course have to convene a meeting of debenture holders so that a resolution may be passed to authorise him to do some of these things. Where the debenture is secured by a fixed charge the charge is given to the trustee since it would not be practicable to give it to a number of debenture holders.

The trustee is appointed at the time when the debentures are issued. Since there are then no debenture holders he is appointed by the company under the terms of the debenture trust deed to which he and the company are both parties. If it is necessary to change the trustee the trust deed usually provides for this appointment to be made by a meeting of the debenture holders.

A receiver and manager for debenture holders may be appointed under a debenture secured by a fixed or floating charge on the company's undertaking and assets. The purpose of the appointment is to enforce the charge by taking control of the assets subject to it. As control of the undertaking will involve carrying on the business, the receiver is also appointed manager. His duty is to secure the payment to the debenture holders of the sums owing to them as principal or interest. If he can achieve this result he will then relinquish his receivership and the directors will resume control.

A receiver and manager is appointed when the company has defaulted under the financial or other terms of the debenture or other prescribed circumstances, e.g. winding up has occurred.

The appointment is usually made by the debenture holders or their trustee (if there is one) under powers given in the trust deed (or under the powers given to a legal mortgagee under the *Law of Property Act 1925*). In the case of difficulty the court will make the appointment (among other circumstances) if the assets charged are in jeopardy by the action of other creditors.

ANSWER B14

As both classes of shares carry equal voting rights the present position is that Smith has 45% and Jones 55% of the votes. Jones cannot carry a special resolution against the opposition of Smith. If, however, Jones can multiply his votes fourfold by dividing his £1 shares into 25p shares, each carrying one vote, he will command a majority in excess of 75%. This would mean that Jones has the voting power to alter the articles as and when he wishes (*s. 10 CA 1948*), a power which cannot be restricted. In this sense Jones's action would be prejudicial to Smith.

If the change proposed were a variation of the rights attached to the preference shares, it would require Smith's consent under the express variation procedure since he holds all those shares.

However, Jones's scheme does not entail any *direct* change in the rights attached to the preference shares. Smith will have 4,500 votes, as before, even though there will be a smaller proportion of the total votes available. Such a change does not amount to a variation of the rights of the preference shares: *Greenhalgh v Arderne Cinemas Ltd* (*1946*), where the facts were similar.

Jones's scheme might however be restrained by the court on a different ground, i.e. that it was an improper use of Jones's powers as controlling shareholder. In *Clemens v Clemens Bros Ltd* (*1976*) the holder of the majority of ordinary shares proposed to issue additional ordinary shares to fellow directors who were likely to support her. The shareholding of the only other holder of ordinary shares would thereby be reduced to less than 25% of the increased issued capital. As this scheme was designed entirely to weaken the position of the minority shareholder and not for the benefit of the company, the court forbade the majority shareholder to use her controlling voting power in this way.

Alternatively, Smith could claim that the affairs of the company are being conducted in an unfairly prejudicial manner: *s. 75 CA 1980*. It would appear that it is no bar to Smith's success that the proposed act by Jones is perfectly constitutional. If Smith were successful the court may make any order it thinks fit, e.g. it could order Jones to purchase Smith's shares at a fair market value.

ANSWER B15

The general principle is that a company cannot reduce its share capital by repaying the shareholders their share capital. *S. 66 CA 1948* is the most important exception to this rule.

The first step is to inspect the articles of association since a reduction of share capital is permitted only if authorised by the articles. If necessary the articles would have to be amended before passing the resolution to reduce share capital. Both resolutions could be taken (in proper sequence) at the same meeting.

At a general meeting of the company a special resolution to reduce share capital in the manner proposed would be passed.

The resolution would then be submitted to the court for confirmation under *s. 67*. An explanation of the reasons for the reduction would be required and also information of the company's financial position as it would be after the reduction.

Where, as in this case, the reduction takes a form, i.e. repayment of cash, which depletes the company's resources available to pay its debts, creditors are entitled to appear at the hearing (in response to advertisement ordered by the court) and object. But the court may dispense with this procedure; it would usually do so if the company could show that it had made arrangements, i.e. by banker's guarantee, to ensure that all its existing debts would be paid.

As there is only one class of shares in this case, the court would not be concerned with how the reduction affects the interests of different classes of shareholders.

If the court is satisfied it would make an order confirming the reduction. A copy of the order is filed at the Companies Registry and the reduction then takes effect: *s. 69*.

The procedure for reduction is the same whether Ash is a private or a public limited company. However, where the court wishes to make an order for reduction of the capital of a public company which would have the effect of bringing it below the authorised minimum of £50,000, the registrar shall not register the reduction unless the court directs or the company is re-registered as a private company: *s. 12 CA 1980*.

ANSWER B16

(a) Two statutory rules have to be kept in view. First, a floating charge ceases to be valid against a liquidator or another creditor if it is not registered at the Companies Registry within 21 days of creation: *s. 95 CA 1948*.

Secondly, if the company goes into liquidation within a year of the creation of a floating charge the charge, even if duly registered, becomes invalid unless it can be shown that the company was solvent at the date of creation. But this rule (*s. 322 CA 1948*) does not apply insofar as it secures money paid to the company after the creation of the charge (plus interest on that sum at the rate of 5% pa).

Accordingly A Ltd should ensure that the floating charge is registered within 21 days of creation and should also postpone paying over the loan until after the charge has been created. Registration is effected by producing the original charge to the Companies Registry with a Form 47 giving brief particulars of the charge. The Registry returns the charge with his certificate of registration and puts the Form 47 on the company's file.

Among other less obvious points A Ltd should ensure that it has power to lend on security, that B Ltd has power to borrow and to give security, and that the purpose of the loan is within the scope of the objects of B Ltd. The charge should be executed under the seal of B Ltd and the sealing witnessed by signatures as required by its articles of association. The charge may also require to be stamped.

(b) A floating charge is an equitable charge which does not attach to specific assets of the borrower until it crystallises. Until that point B Ltd is free to dispose of its assets without A Ltd having any claim on those specific assets as security.

A floating charge crystallises on the happening of any act of default specified as such in the charge. Apart from failure to pay interest or to repay the loan when due, a charge would usually specify such occurrences as the company ceasing to trade or defaulting in payment of its debts to trade creditors. In such a case the lender would take steps to enforce his security and the charge would crystallise. The charge also crystallises on the appointment of a receiver and on the company going into liquidation.

When the charge crystallises it attaches to the assets then owned by the company, but in a liquidation any preferential debts would be paid out of those assets in priority to the claims of the holder of the charge.

ANSWER B17

(a) Subject to relaxations introduced by *CA 1981*, a company may never acquire its own shares by purchase even if it has power in its articles: *Trevor v Whitworth (1887)*—now *s. 35 CA 1980*. A company may acquire its own fully paid shares otherwise than for valuable consideration or on a reduction of capital under *s. 66 CA 1948*. A company may even be ordered to purchase its own shares under *s. 75 CA 1980*. These basic rules remain substantially the same, but *CA 1981* permits companies (subject to consent in their articles):

(1) to issue redeemable *equity* shares, which entails a repeal of *s. 58 CA 1948* and an extension of the principle of that section that a company may redeem such shares from profits on creation of a capital redemption reserve or a new issue of shares made for the purpose;

(2) subject to safeguards and publicity to purchase any of their own shares as described in (1); and

(3) in the case of *private companies only*, to redeem or purchase such shares (subject to stringent safeguards) from capital where distributable profits are not adequate.

(b) There is a general prohibition imposed by *s. 42 CA 1981* on a company financing the purchase of its own shares but an exception is where lending money is part of the ordinary business, e.g. where a bank lends money to a customer for general investment and he uses part of it to buy a holding in shares of the bank. This is a twofold test:

(i) Is the loan part of the ordinary business of the creditor?

(ii) Was the loan made in the ordinary course of business? (*Fowlie v Slater* (*1979*)). For other exceptions, see answer B4.

(c) A company must have an express power in its objects clause to hold shares of another company; the power will not be implied. Apart from that there is no restriction.

(d) A company may be a director of another company and does not require an express power to that effect in its objects clause. It can only be the *sole* director provided that the other company is a private company (public companies require a minimum of two directors), that the articles of the other company do not set a larger minimum than one director, and that the director company is not also secretary nor has itself a sole director who is secretary of the other company: *s. 178 CA 1948*.

(e) A corporate body may never be liquidator of another company: *s. 335 CA 1948*. The same rule applies to receiverships.

ANSWER B18

(a) On the appointment of a receiver, whether by the debenture holders or by the court, of the whole of a company's undertaking as in this case, the directors of the company are required by *s. 372 CA 1948* to submit to the receiver within 14 days of being informed of his appointment a statement of affairs showing the assets and liabilities of the company with particulars of its creditors and of the security (if any) which they hold: *s. 373 CA 1948*. Peter and Henry therefore have work to do for the receiver quite apart from answering his questions. If the receiver had been appointed to deal with only one specific asset no statement of affairs would be required.

(b) The appointment of a receiver by the debenture holder, as in this case, does not automatically terminate the contracts of employment of the company's staff (although it would do so if the receiver had been appointed by the court). This is the position even though he is appointed receiver of the company's whole undertaking. Paul has not yet lost his job with the company though the receiver has power to dismiss him if he sees fit. Paul would do best to wait to meet the receiver: *Reid v Explosives Co* (*1887*).

(c) The appointment of a receiver suspends the powers of the directors because the receiver takes the management of the company's business out of their hands: *Reid's Case* above. This is so even if the receiver is appointed by the debenture holder and not by the court: *Re Foster Clark* (*1966*). It is pointless for the company secretary to make preparations for a board meeting to deal with routine business. The directors do however retain powers to act to protect the interests of the company in matters with which the receiver is not concerned or against the debenture holder whom the receiver represents: *Newhart Developments Ltd v Co-operative Commercial Bank Ltd* (*1978*).

ANSWER B19

The articles of association of a company have effect as a contract made between its members and the company in respect of membership rights: *s. 20 CA 1948*. The company may have an express variation of class rights procedure stated in its articles along the lines of *Table A Article 4*, i.e. the class rights may be varied by three fourths of the holders of that class of shares given in writing or three quarters of the votes cast at a class meeting. In the absence of express provision, *s. 32 CA 1980* provides that class rights set out in the articles can only be varied with the consent of three fourths of the shareholders of that class as in *Article 4*. In either case Paul and Tom have the voting rights to alter the articles to make the preference shares non-cumulative and reduce the rate to 6%.

To safeguard a minority of members holding shares of one class in circumstances such as these, *s. 72 CA 1948* provides that the holder or holders of not less than 15% of the shares of a class whose rights are to be varied may apply to the court within 21 days for cancellation of the variation. The court must either confirm or cancel the variation, i.e. it cannot (as with objections to an alteration of objects) impose some compromise or alternative. The sole ground on which the court may disallow the variation is that 'it is satisfied that the variation would unfairly prejudice the shareholders of the class represented'.

There might well be such unfairness here. It was held in *Re Holder's Investment Trust Ltd* (*1972*) that consent procured by shareholders' votes was unfair if those shareholders were in fact voting for their own selfish interests as members of another class; they should vote *bona fide* for the benefit of the class as such. Here, Paul and Tom, in supporting the variation, are clearly benefiting themselves as ordinary shareholders to the detriment of the preference shareholders.

James should be advised to make an application under *s. 72 CA 1948*.

ANSWER B20

(a) If its articles so provide a company may (*s. 61 CA 1948*) cancel any unissued shares. The procedure prescribed by the articles must be followed and a copy of any resolution (and also a copy of the memorandum showing the change in the share capital clause) must be filed at the Companies Registry: *ss. 61–62 CA 1948: s. 9 ECA 1972*. Under *Table A Article 45*, unissued shares may be cancelled by ordinary resolution.

(b) The repayment of part of money paid as subscription for issued shares is a reduction of share capital to which *ss. 66–69 CA 1948* apply.

There must be authority in the articles (in this case *Table A Article 46*) and a special resolution must be passed in general meeting: (*s. 66*). Application is then made to the court for approval and the relevant financial information to show that the company can afford to repay

£30,000 is produced. Creditors have a right to object if the reduction consists of a diminution of liability or a return of paid-up share capital, as in this case. The court is required (*s. 67*) to consider the effect of the repayment on the company's creditors. Unless some bankers guarantee or other adequate security is obtained to ensure that all existing creditors will be paid in full, the court will order an advertisement to be published and will later consider any objections raised by creditors.

If the court is satisfied that the interests of creditors are safeguarded it will make an order approving the reduction. The order is produced to the Registrar of Companies with a 'minute' setting out the details of the change of capital. The reduction takes effect and the cash may be paid out as soon as the court order is registered.

The court may require the words 'and reduced' to be added to the company's name but in practice this is not usually done.

As there is only one class of shares in this case, the court is not concerned, whereas it would be if there were more than one class, with class rights in respect of capital and its repayment.

If Zed were a new public company, such a reduction as proposed in (b) would reduce the company's share capital below the authorised minimum for a public company—i.e. £50,000. The registrar must not register such a reduction unless the company first re-registers as a private company: *s. 12 CA 1980*.

ANSWER B21

The grant of Stock Exchange permission to deal in securities increases their marketability and therefore greatly increases their market price. Accordingly a prospectus may, and in practice always does, announce that as soon as the issue has been made, application will be made for a Stock Exchange quotation; the price at which the shares or debentures are offered to the public is fixed on the assumption that a quotation will be obtained; hence the prospective subscriber must be protected against the loss which he would suffer if quotation were refused and the value of the shares allotted to him was thereby reduced.

S. 51 CA 1948 provides that no allotment may be made in such a case unless application has been made to the Stock Exchange before the third day after the issue of the prospectus. Any allotment in breach of this rule is void.

Secondly, *s. 51* in effect requires that a quotation shall be obtained within 21 days after the closing of the subscription lists or such longer period not exceeding 42 days as the Stock Exchange may allow. If quotation is not obtained or is refused within that period any allotment made becomes void and all subscription moneys must be returned within eight days of the allotment becoming void. If repayment is not duly made the directors become personally liable to repay the money with interest at 5% pa.

ANSWER B22

(a) A floating charge ranks behind a fixed charge on any of the same assets if the fixed charge was made first (as in the facts of the question) and was properly registered. But a floating charge over 'undertaking and assets' takes in all assets fixed or current. Accordingly the floating charge offered to George will apply to (i) any surplus value of the factory ('the equity of redemption') remaining after the bank's fixed charge has been discharged by repayment, (ii) to the plant and vehicles, and (iii) to the current assets of the company; in all cases the assets available will be those at the time of crystallisation of the floating charge.

(b) The main risks are that the company may subsequently create additional fixed charges over its fixed assets ranking before the floating charge (it is possible but difficult for George to prevent this); secondly, the current assets of the company may be much reduced in value from their present level when the floating charge later attaches to them on crystallisation; and thirdly, the preferential debts of the company will be paid out of the assets subject to the floating charge as there can in this case be no other assets from which those debts can be paid. A judgement creditor and a landlord who has distrained for rent owing will also have priority claims: *s. 319(5) and (7)*: *s. 325 CA 1948*. There is also a risk that a floating charge may be invalidated under *s. 322 CA 1948* but not if given for cash introduced at the time of the charge or later, as should be the case here.

ANSWER B23

A company is obliged to maintain its share capital for the benefit of its creditors. The share capital is the fund to which the creditors can properly look for the satisfaction of their debts. A company may not reduce its capital unless it uses the statutory procedure in *ss. 66–69 CA 1948*. If a company purchases its own shares, this might lead to a reduction of the capital available to the creditors. Similarly if a company is allowed to provide financial assistance to another in connection with a purchase of the company's own shares, this would also be objectionable (*s. 42 CA 1981*). The prohibition on a company providing financial assistance for its own shares was introduced to complement and prevent evasion of the normal company law rule in *Trevor v Whitworth* (*1887*) that a company cannot purchase its own shares (*s. 35 CA 1980* puts this rule into statutory form although there are some relaxations in *CA 1981*).

S. 42 provides that a company may not give financial assistance (which includes a gift, loan or guarantee) whether directly or indirectly to enable a person to acquire shares in the company or assist in the discharge of a liability incurred as a result of that acquisition.

The test stipulated by this provision is—what was the purpose of the transaction? If that purpose was to give financial assistance for the acquisition of shares it is unlawful, the form the transaction may take being immaterial. Thus it may be unlawful to buy an asset from a person to provide him with money which he needs and uses to buy shares of the company.

The following are declared not to infringe the prohibition whether the company is public or private:

(i) A company is permitted to give financial assistance if acting in good faith and the principal purpose in giving the assistance is not the acquisition of its shares, but an incidental part of some larger purpose of the company.
(ii) Loans in the ordinary course of business by a company whose ordinary business is lending money (if the company knows the purpose of the loan it is questionable whether it could be in the ordinary course of that company's business).
(iii) Money provided for the acquisition of shares in accordance with an employees' share scheme or loans to employees other than directors enabling them to acquire shares in the company.
(iv) Legitimate distributions by way of dividends, distributions in the course of winding up, allotment of bonus shares or any arrangement made in accordance with various statutory provisions regulating agreements with creditors or as a result of court orders.

Private companies

Whilst reaffirming the rule that it is unlawful for a company or its subsidiaries to give financial assistance for the purchase of its shares, the Act introduced a procedure by which, subject to safeguards, a private company might lawfully give financial assistance for the acquisition of its shares or those of its holding company (provided it is also a private company). The following provisions must be complied with:

(i) The company must have net assets which are not thereby reduced or, to the extent that they are reduced, the financial assistance must be provided out of distributable profits.
(ii) The assistance must be approved by a special resolution.
(iii) The directors are required to make a statutory declaration giving details of the assistance and certifying that in their opinion the company can pay its debts and will continue to be able to do so during the ensuing 12 months. This must be supported by a report made by the auditors confirming that the directors' conclusions are reasonable.
(iv) Holders of 10% of the company's issued share capital or any class thereof may apply to the court to cancel the resolution authorising the assistance.

The above provisions are intended to protect minority shareholders and creditors, but note that creditors do not have a right to object to the court.

ANSWER B24

When W Plc makes an offer for all the issued shares of T Plc there is no rule of law to prevent W from acquiring all or any of T's shares by purchase on the Stock Exchange at a higher price. Those of T's shareholders who sell through the Stock Exchange and W as purchaser are not impeded by the existence of an alternative opportunity of sale in response to the take-over bid.

This practice is however considered unfair to those of T's members who do not obtain the benefit of selling at the higher price. Accordingly the City Code of Takeovers and Mergers requires that the price offered in a take-over bid shall if necessary be increased to the highest price at which the bidder has purchased shares through the market during the period of his take-over bid. Jack should therefore report the facts to the Panel which enforces the Code (by extra-legal sanctions such as the threat of suspending Stock Exchange quotation of the bidder's shares).

Ss. 191–194 CA 1948 contain rules to prevent the payment to directors of compensation for loss of office unless such payments have been approved by shareholders in general meeting. To prevent evasion of the main rule in a take-over, *s. 193* requires that where an offer is made to the general body of shareholders for their shares the directors of the company must secure that the offer document discloses any proposed compensation for loss of office. *S. 194* provides that any price paid to directors for their shares (within two years before or one year after the take-over bid) shall to the extent of the margin of any excess price above the price available to shareholders generally be treated as a compensation payment to the directors.

Jack should require the facts to be disclosed and submitted for approval in general meeting. If the directors fail in this duty they are liable to be fined and the excess over the general offer price received by them is a sum held in trust for shareholders who have sold their shares.

ANSWER B25

The appointment of Ibbotson as receiver by the debenture holders does not of itself affect any contracts of the company existing at the date of his appointment. If however he had been appointed by the court this event would have terminated the contracts of service of the company's employees: *Reid v Explosives Co* (*1887*). But Ibbotson has retained the employees in service and performed the existing trade contracts. He is not liable on those contracts but has personal liability for any new contracts he may have made for the company since his appointment: *s. 369*(*2*) *CA 1948*.

If he arranges a bank loan, that is a new contract on which he will be personally liable. In principle he is the agent of the debenture holders who appointed him but they have (as is the normal practice) provided in the debentures that any receiver is to be the agent of the company. If therefore he is to assume personal liability by raising a loan for the company he should require the debenture holders to indemnify him in case his indemnity from the company under *s. 369* is inadequate.

If he sells the business the sale will operate as a termination of the company's contracts of employment with its staff. They will have claims against the company for breach of contract and for statutory compensation. If of course the receiver can arrange for the purchaser to offer similar employment to the company's staff they will (broadly speaking) have no substantial claims against the company. He might first transfer the business assets and the employees to a new wholly-owned subsidiary and then sell the shares of the subsidiary; this is a common practice.

A receiver can terminate existing contracts but if doing so will injure the company's goodwill he must obtain leave of the court. To close down the business and terminate all contracts would clearly fall under this rule. The court would require to be satisfied that there was no reasonable alternative before it gave its leave. The court would grant its leave as requested rather than compel the receiver to borrow money (with personal liability).

ANSWER B26

An aggrieved person who has successfully applied for shares on the strength of a prospectus which, it transpires, contained a material misrepresentation of fact, may have the following three courses open to him with a view to obtaining a remedy.

(i) To rescind the contract. This is an equitable remedy taken against the company, the plaintiff claiming the return of his money with interest. To succeed he must show that the misrepresentation was one of material fact and not opinion, and that he acted upon it, although it need not have been the sole cause of his entering into the contract. Non-disclosure of a material fact may amount to a misrepresentation if the remainder is misleading without that fact: *Coles v White City Greyhound Stadium* (*1929*). Further, if the misrepresentation is in a report actually included in the prospectus the contract can be rescinded unless the company specificially stated that it did not vouch for the accuracy of the report. The plaintiff must note that the right to rescind will be lost if:

(a) he waives the right to rescind by acting as a member of the company after discovering that the prospectus is untrue or even by failing to act with reasonable speed in rescinding after the discovery. Attending and voting at a company meeting; receiving and retaining a dividend; or attempting to sell the shares might amount to waiver by exercise of membership rights;

(b) the company goes into liquidation since its assets are then held to meet the claims of its creditors:

(c) the member cannot restore to the company the shares allocated to him because he has sold or transferred them.

(ii) To claim damages for fraud. If he rescinds, the plaintiff may also have an action for damages for fraud against the directors or promoters, the amount claimable being the difference between the actual value of the shares and the amount paid for them. To succeed in this action for the tort of deceit he must prove that the defendants authorised the issue of a prospectus containing a statement of fact which they knew to be false, or which they made recklessly, regardless of its truth or otherwise: *Derry v Peek (1889)*. The statement must have been made with the intention that another person should act upon it, and the plaintiff must have so acted to his subsequent detriment.

(iii) To claim statutory compensation. An alternative action to claiming damages for fraud would be to claim compensation from any director, promoter or other person authorising the issue of a prospectus which contains an untrue statement, even if made innocently: *s. 43 CA 1948*. The plaintiff must show that he subscribed for shares on the strength of such a statement. The measure of compensation is the same as the measure of damages outlined above. The onus is on the defendant to establish one of the statutory defences set out in the section: in effect to show he had reasonable grounds for his statements—if he cannot do so he must compensate the plaintiff.

ANSWER B27

(a) The first scheme was not possible so far as concerns the shares in Porter because it is a settled principle of company law that a company cannot purchase its own shares as this would lead to a reduction of capital: *Trevor v Whitworth (1887)*—now *s. 35 CA 1980*. The rules are now relaxed, however, by *CA 1981* and as from 1 June 1982 a private company, if it follows the stringent rules set out in the Act may purchase its own shares even out of capital, if it has insufficient distributable profits out of which to do so. Essentially, members and creditors are protected in the last resort by being able to apply to the court for relief if they object to the purchase. There is nothing to prevent Porter from buying the debentures belonging to A unless the debentures were issued on terms which prohibit this step.

(b) It is not lawful in principle for Porter to guarantee a loan in connection with the purchase of shares in the company: *s. 42 CA 1981*. There are several permitted exceptions to the rules especially where a private company is involved. If the provisions of the Act are followed a private company may give financial assistance to acquire the shares for any purpose. Porter could however guarantee a loan made to B in connection with the purchase of debentures provided the stringent provisions of *CA 1981* are adhered to.

(c) Again, there is no objection to the loan for the purchase of the shares or debentures if the provisions of *CA 1981* are followed. For these provisions, see answer B23.

ANSWER B28

(a) A person becomes a member of a company in any of four situations.

First, a subscriber to the memorandum of association states the number of shares, usually only one, which he agrees to take and pay for on the incorporation of the company: *s. 26 CA 1948*. He becomes a member as soon as the certificate of incorporation is issued and an entry in the register of members is not necessary to make him a member. It is the duty of the directors, however, to enter his name in the register but their failure to do so does not enable him to escape liability for money due on his subscription shares. It is not correct for the directors to allot the shares to him. But if they allot all the available shares to others he is discharged from his liability in respect of subscribers' shares: *Mackley's Case (1875)*.

Secondly, directors who have signed and delivered to the Registrar of Companies an undertaking to take their qualification shares are in the same position as subscribers to the memorandum of association: *s. 182(1) CA 1948*.

Thirdly, any person becomes a member if (i) he has agreed to this and (ii) his name has been entered in the register of members: *s. 26(2) CA 1948*. A person who, for example, applies to the company for the issue of shares or who presents for registration a transfer of shares to himself thereby expresses his agreement but does not become a member until his name is entered in the register. A person to whom shares have been allotted under a renounceable letter of allotment does not become a member until his name is entered in the register. Another person to whom he may transfer his letter of allotment will become a member on registration and the original allottee is then not a member at any time.

Finally, a person may be liable as a member by the operation of estoppel if he allows himself to remain on the register as a shareholder when he is not a shareholder.

A personal representative or a trustee in bankruptcy of a member may himself become a member but is not automatically a member by virtue of his position.

(b) A person who has been a member of a company ceases to be a member when a transfer of all the shares which he holds on the register to other person(s) is entered in the register. The company is required to enter in the register the date on which any person ceases to be a member: *s. 110(1)(c) CA 1948*.

On the death of a member the shares registered in his name (as sole shareholder) are part of his estate until the personal representatives either replace him or transfer the shares to a third party. But the deceased member is no longer a member in any personal sense; he would not, for example, be counted under the rules on minimum membership: *s. 31 CA 1948*. Transmission of shares also occurs on bankruptcy.

A person may also cease to be a member if his name is removed from the register to correct a mistaken entry. Any person may apply to the court for an order for rectification of the register by, among other things, removal of his name from the register: *s. 116 CA 1948*. The company might also remove his name without an order of the court but it is doubtful whether this is a correct and valid procedure.

Surrender, forfeiture, redemption or purchase of the shares by the company also brings membership to an end, as does dissolution of the company.

ANSWER B29

(a) The various class rights of the shareholders are presumably stated in the company's articles of association. This first proposal by the company amounts to a variation of class rights. If the company's articles are along the lines of *Table A, Article 4* states that a company may only vary its class rights with the consent of a three-quarters majority resolution of the members of that class given in writing or three-quarters of the votes cast at a class meeting. *S. 32 CA 1980* now provides that where a company has no express variation clause requiring class contents, class rights can only be varied if three-quarters of the members of that class consent in writing to the variation or an extraordinary resolution is passed at a separate meeting of the members of that class.

Henry, however, only holds 1,000 out of 5,000 preference shares, so if the others agree to the variation (which they might do if for example they also hold ordinary shares), he could not prevent the reduction in dividend. He could avail himself of *s. 72 CA 1948* which provides that 15% of the holders of a class of shares may apply to the court within 21 days to have the variation cancelled. Henry should do this but he cannot do so if he voted in favour of the variation.

The court may disallow the variation if it is satisfied having regard to all the circumstances that the variation would unfairly prejudice the shareholders applying for cancellation.

If Henry failed under *s. 72 CA 1948* he could complain to the court under *s. 75 CA 1980* that the proposed action of the company would be unfairly prejudicial to him but similar considerations would apply under either section.

(b) As long as the company offers these shares to the existing ordinary shareholders in proportion to their holding it complies with *s. 17 CA 1980*. The preference shareholders do not get the benefit of pre-emption rights in respect of a different class of shares. The preference shareholders could not object to the issue of unissued shares on the basis of a variation of class rights, as although it reduces their effective voting strength it does not alter or vary their class rights—it merely affects their enjoyment of the shares. *A fortiori*, Henry could not claim that this was a variation: *White v Bristol Aeroplane Co* (*1953*).

Henry could possibly claim that this constitutes a fraud on the minority as in *Clemens v Clemens Bros Ltd* (*1976*) where the court prohibited a company from issuing new shares which were deliberately intended to *water down* the voting rights of another member; or he could claim it to be unfairly prejudicial conduct under *s. 75 CA 1980.*

(c) This would involve a reduction of capital under *s. 66 CA 1948*. If the preference shareholders have no priority as to repayment of capital on a liquidation (and none is stated in the question) the presumption of equality applies and the preference shareholders and ordinary shareholders should be paid off rateably: *Re Mackenzie & Co* (*1916*). If the preference shareholders have a right to repayment of capital in priority to the shareholders, they must be paid off first on a reduction of capital under *s. 66 CA 1948*. They cannot complain that this is a variation of class rights as the company is merely doing what the articles authorise: *Re Saltdean Estates Co Ltd* (*1968*). Henry could merely inform the court of his objections to the proposals when the scheme for reduction is considered by the court. If the ordinary shareholders hold the rest of the preference shares, the court may decide that the decision to reduce was not taken in the best interest of the preference shareholders.

ANSWER B30

The purpose of creating a floating charge is usually to create a charge over current assets which by their nature cannot be made subject to a fixed charge.

The accepted description of a floating charge was given in *Re Yorkshire Woolcombers Association Ltd* (*1903*) as follows:

(a) it is a charge on a class of assets, both present and future;
(b) it is a charge on a class of assets which in the ordinary course of the company's business will change from time to time;
(c) it is the intention that until the charge attaches to assets by crystallisation the company may dispose of or deal with the assets in the ordinary course of its business. This includes, the right of the company to sell its undertaking and to create fixed charges over its assets (unless expressly prohibited from doing so).

The floating charge crystallises if the company defaults in payment of interest or repayment of principal of the loan or if the debenture holders, for whom the charge has been created, take action in prescribed circumstances to enforce their security, usually by appointing a receiver. Crystallisation also occurs if the company goes into liquidation (even a members' liquidation for purposes of reconstruction) or possibly if it ceases to carry on its business. It is probably possible to insert clauses to ensure 'automatic crystallisation' in the event of default.

The effect of a floating charge is therefore to give the holders of the charge a right by way of security to the assets charged whatever they may be at the time of crystallisation but their rights do not prevent the company from dealing with the assets in the course of business until the charge crystallises. It follows that a fixed charge created after a floating charge can rank in priority to it since a fixed charge will usually attach to the asset charged as soon as the charge is created. This issue only arises when both the charges apply to fixed assets. Priorities may, however, be adversely affected by failure to register under *s. 95 CA 1948.*

When the holders of a floating charge enforce it they have the normal rights of a secured creditor over the assets charged, but unlike a fixed charge this is subject to the claims of any preferential creditors.

A floating charge is usually created in express terms by a clause of a secured debenture issued under the seal of the company. But it can be created informally, e.g. by instructing trade debtors of the company to pay their debts to a bank (*Kent & Sussex Sawmills* (*1942*)) or by purchasing goods on the basis that the seller shall retain the beneficial ownership of the goods until he is paid (*Re Bond Worth Ltd* (*1979*)). A company which makes a large-scale issue of debentures or debenture stock often does so through the medium of a debenture trust deed. Under this deed, the company appoints a trustee who is given a charge (often a floating charge) on the assets covered and who has the power to exercise the appropriate remedies on behalf of the debenture holders.

ANSWER B31

Bridge is a private limited company. There are a number of restrictions imposed on such a company when issuing new shares.

(i) It must only issue up to the authorised amount of its share capital unless it also obtains an increase of share capital: *s. 61 CA 1948.*

(ii) Usually, the power is given to the directors to issue shares but they must also have authority from the shareholders either in the articles or by a resolution of a general meeting to allot the shares: *s. 14 CA 1980.*

(iii) The company must first offer the shares to the existing shareholders in proportion to their existing holdings: *s. 17 CA 1980.*

(iv) The company must not offer its shares to the public: *s. 15 CA 1980.*

(a) This proposed issue is up the authorised amount of the company's share capital; thus it does not involve any increase of the authorised share capital. However, the price of 80p is a 20p discount on the nominal value, i.e. £1 of the share and contrary to *s. 21 CA 1980.* If the shares were issued at this discount they would be valid but treated as partly paid up shares and the 'discount' would remain a liability of the allottee. Moreover, it could be evidence of a breach of the directors' duty always to act in the best interest of the company, i.e. to obtain the best price possible on the shares, but as the company is experiencing financial difficulties it may be that the market price is even less than 80p.

It might be advisable for the company to issue debentures instead of shares as these can be issued at a discount.

(b) Two additional points arise here. Firstly, the proposed issue involves an increase in share capital of £10,000. The company would need to

(i) have the power to increase its capital in its articles or to change the articles giving itself the necessary power;

(ii) pass the necessary resolution (ordinary or special depending on the company's articles): *s. 61 CA 1948*;

(iii) register the details of the increase with the Registrar.

Secondly, the shares are to be issued at a premium of 20p per share. The premium must be put into a separate share premium account and used only for the purposes specified in *s. 56 CA 1948*. Share premium is for most purposes treated as share capital and constitutes part of the company's undistributable reserves—it cannot be used for paying a dividend.

ANSWER B32

The appointment of a receiver is one means by which secured creditors (this remedy is not available to unsecured creditors) obtain control of the assets charged to them with a view to payment being made from the income or realised proceeds of those assets.

If the creditors have a floating charge over the *undertaking* of the company the receiver will also be (or may be assisted by) a manager since the receiver has to run the business.

A receiver and manager is normally appointed by the debenture holders or their trustees under powers given in the debenture (or trust deed). The appointment may be made when the company has made default in payment of loan capital or interest or in such other circumstances as are specified in the debenture. It is usually provided that the receiver is to be an agent of the company and not of those who appointed him.

If it is not possible to make the appointment under the terms of the debenture, application may be made to the court for the appointment of a receiver and manager. It must then be shown either that the company is in financial default on the debenture, or that it has begun to be wound up, or that the assets subject to the charge are *in jeopardy*, e.g. because the company is about to close down its business, or to dispose of its assets, or that other creditors are threatening to sue for debt or to petition for winding up. The court will not generally appoint a receiver and manager for a longer period than three months to permit sale of the business.

Notice of the appointment must be given to the Registrar of Companies within seven days and it must be shown on the company's letterheads: *ss. 102 and 370 CA 1948*.

ANSWER B33

A floating charge is one of the types of charge which must be registered in the company's own records according to *ss. 103/105 CA 1948*. A copy of every instrument creating a charge on the company's property must also be kept at the company's registered office with the register of charges. There are provisions in the Act providing for inspection by members and other persons. If this is not done, the officer of the company who is in default is subject to a default fine but non-registration does not affect the validity of the charge.

Such a charge also has to be registered under *s. 95 CA 1948* (as do most other charges on the assets of companies). This is not registration in the company's own records but with the Registrar of Companies. The effects of non-registration are serious. If the charge is not registered within 21 days after its creation *s. 95* provides that it will be void against the liquidator and any creditor of the company. If this happens the creditor loses his security and is reduced to the status of an ordinary creditor. Moreover, any money secured by the charge is immediately repayable by the company. Apart from these serious effects upon the company and the lender, *s. 96* imposes a default fine on the company for not registering the charge. The unregistered charge will be valid against the unsecured creditors until such time as a winding up commences. The section in effect applies to make a charge void against the liquidator *on behalf of* the unsecured creditors. Until a liquidation occurs they have acquired no proprietary rights. Until liquidation, therefore, the holder of the charge may deal with the property on the basis of his security. It is only on a liquidation that he loses that security and ranks as an ordinary creditor.

Any other secured creditors, however, who register their charges will thereby obtain priority over an unregistered charge. Non-registration may therefore seriously affect the priority between the holders of several charges on the same property.

It is possible to register out of time with the leave of the court as provided by *s. 101 CA 1948* but leave will usually only be given on the basis that any rights which have been acquired by third parties in the meantime will not be prejudiced. Once the company has gone into liquidation it is too late to seek registration out of time.

The facts set out in the question do not suggest any defect in registration of Brown's floating charge. It is therefore assumed there is none. It is apparent that A Ltd is in financial difficulty but has nevertheless been complying with the terms of the debenture and paying Brown his interest. Can he in these circumstances enforce the security? This depends principally upon the terms of the debenture. Clearly, if the debenture permits it Brown's best course will be to appoint a receiver. This will cause the floating charge to crystallise and prevent unsecured creditors like the trade creditors and the landlord from obtaining a proprietary interest in the company's assets. This they might do in the case of trade creditors by obtaining judgements against A Ltd and levying execution on its assets or in the case of the landlord by distraining for the unpaid rent.

Much depends on the precise terms of the debenture. It may well contain clauses stipulating when the floating charge will crystallise and it may give power to appoint a receiver or receiver and manager. Relying on the debenture, therefore, Brown may be able to appoint a receiver without needing to apply to the court. An appointment out of court is clearly time saving and money saving and most well drawn floating charges will cover the point adequately. Even if the floating charge does not stipulate that a receiver may be appointed, provided it is by deed an implied power to appoint a receiver is conferred by *s. 101* of the *Law of Property Act 1925*.

If, however, the terms of the debenture are not satisfactory and it is not under seal there will be no power to appoint a receiver out of court. In that event an application must be made to the court. The court may appoint a receiver under a debenture when the principal or interest is in arrear or when the company is being wound up or the security is in jeopardy. Here the principal or interest is not in arrear. It may be that creditors may take action for winding up but that has not yet occurred. Is the security in jeopardy? Numerous cases have been decided concerning the meaning of jeopardy and it is clear that the expression includes various situations in which the company's property is in danger of being taken by creditors or others over whom the debenture ought to have priority.

This would include situations where execution is about to be levied or where the company proposes to distribute its assets to members. The same would apply where creditors are threatening to wind up the company and the company has ceased to carry on business in circumstances involving pressure from creditors. It may well be that Brown can prove that the company is insolvent which means that it is unable to meet its debts as they fall due. Some evidence to establish one of these situations will be necessary before the court will make an order. It may be easy for Brown to prove that the creditors are threatening some action which could result in the levying of execution or that the landlord is preparing to distrain for the outstanding rent.

The appointment of a receiver is not to be confused with the appointment of a liquidator. The company need not necessarily go into liquidation merely because a receiver is appointed. A receiver is appointed to safeguard the position of an individual debenture holder and to obtain repayment of the money lent on the security of the debenture. His task is not to wind up the company and very often he will in fact save the company. Clearly by restoring it to health he improves the chances of the debenture holder receiving repayment in full.

Brown should be advised accordingly.

ANSWER B34

(a) The articles are the company's rules for internal government, and the Companies Act allows substantial freedom in altering them. Limitations placed on this freedom by the Act and by the courts in their interpretation of the Act, are aimed at ensuring that it is not fettered and not abused. Limitations placed for this purpose include the following:

(i) A provision in the articles, or amendment to the articles, prohibiting any further alteration is void. Similarly, a provision would be void which allowed only those who were against an amendment of the articles to vote on it.

(ii) The articles cannot be altered to produce an inconsistency with the memorandum.

(iii) Under *s. 22 CA 1948* a member cannot be obliged, by alteration of the memorandum or articles, to take more shares than he held at the date of the alteration or otherwise to increase his liability without his written consent.

(iv) If under *s. 75 CA 1980* the court orders an alteration of the articles in order to relieve a petitioner from prejudicial conduct then further inconsistent alterations may not be made without the court's consent.

(v) The court may restrain or set aside any alterations which are not *bona fide* for the benefit of the company as a whole. The decision as to what is for the benefit of the company as a whole is one which is primarily for the members, provided they act in good faith. A member is not precluded from voting on the amendment simply because he will benefit by it. The law reports contain a number of examples where the alteration is such that it will diminish the expectations of the complainant; but that of itself does not invalidate the alteration. In *Shuttleworth v Cox Bros & Co (Maidenhead) Ltd (1927)* for example, the court found that an alteration which would enable the company to dismiss an unsatisfactory director appointed for life was one which had been made in an honest endeavour to act for the benefit of the company.

In *Greenhalgh v Arderne Cinemas Ltd (1946)* an alteration which in effect deprived the complainant of his expectation to take the company over by exercising his right of pre-emption was upheld, particularly on the grounds that it was not discriminatory.

Equally, the courts have refused to allow an alteration when its effect *has* been shown to be discriminatory. In *Brown v British Abrasive Wheel Co (1919)* the majority were prepared to supply further capital provided they could take over shares of a minority who were not prepared to invest further. The articles were altered to give a power of compulsory purchase. The court restrained the company from making the alteration, on the ground that it was not done *bona fide* for the benefit of the company as a whole. On the other hand, in *Sidebottom v Kershaw, Leese & Co Ltd (1920)* the insertion of a similar expropriation clause was upheld because it applied only to shareholders in competition with the company and was therefore *bona fide* for the benefit of the company.

(b) The question posed by this problem is whether the proposed alteration is *bona fide* for the benefit of the company as a whole, or whether it is discriminatory against John and Paul.

(i) It is not objectionable simply because it will benefit the majority (who, as fully paid shareholders, will take a proportionately higher number of shares on any future bonus issue). The company could already achieve this situation indirectly by always paying cash dividends and then offering shares to its members for cash (although that might not be possible in a time of dividend restraint imposed by the government).

(ii) In *Greenhalgh v Arderne Cinemas Ltd*, the court suggested that the test was to take an individual hypothetical member and ask whether what was proposed was, in the honest opinion of the majority, for that person's benefit. If that question is asked here, it would appear that the answer would be 'Yes'. The individual hypothetical member would presumably desire equality of treatment, rather than privilege for one group of partly paid up members.

(iii) John and Paul, in becoming members, must be taken to have realised that they might be called upon to pay up their shares in full: it can therefore hardly be discriminatory against them to require them (in effect) to do so as a condition of receiving the same benefits as fully paid up shareholders. Indeed, in *Allen v Gold Reefs of West Africa Ltd* (*1900*) it was held that a company could alter its articles to extend a lien to all shares (even those fully paid) for debts already incurred because this was *bona fide* for the company's benefit.

John and Paul should therefore be advised that the courts would be unlikely to disallow the alteration. On similar facts, an Australian decision was arrived at to that effect, although of course this is only of persuasive authority in the UK.

ANSWER B35

(i) A variation of class rights will only occur where there is a direct attack on those rights, as where dividends are reduced or direct voting power is revoked or reduced by directly taking away benefits attached to shares of the class concerned. It is not such a variation if instead of a direct attack there is a mere creation of new rights in other people than an alteration of existing rights.

The facts here resemble in substance those in *White v Bristol Aeroplane Co* (*1953*) in which it was held that the dilution of the voting power of the existing preference share by the issue of more was not a variation of class rights.

Here Fred possesses class rights, but on the basis of the decided cases, although his enjoyment of those rights has been affected, the rights themselves remain exactly as they were before. There has been no variation and Fred cannot apply to the court for protection under *s. 72 CA 1948*, which applies only when there has been a variation.

'Preference shares are not "equity securities" and Fred will not therefore have the benefit of the pre-emption rights conferred by *s. 17 CA 1980*.'

(ii) Relief for oppressed minorities was under *s. 210 CA 1948* the 'alternative remedy' to a winding up order on the 'just and equitable' ground under *s. 222*(*f*). Unless the petitioner was entitled to a winding up order he could not obtain a *s. 210* order to bring to an end the oppression complained of. The section was minimally used by the courts and they insisted that a course of conduct, and not just an isolated act oppressing the petitioner in his capacity as a member (not for example as an employee—*Elder v Elder and Watson Ltd* (*1952*)) was burdensome, harsh and wrongful. The only two successful reported cases are *Re H R Harmer Ltd* (*1959*) and *Scottish Co-operative Wholesale Society Ltd v Meyer* (*1959*). A mere business decision (e.g.

non-payment of dividends as in *Re Jermyn Street Turkish Baths Ltd* (*1971*) or negligence or incompetence (as in *Re Five Minute Car Wash Service Ltd* (*1966*)) would not suffice. Usually *s. 210* was placed as a second line of attack to a petition for winding up. Under *s. 222* (*f*) the just and equitable ground for winding up has been held to include cases of breakdown in the mutual trust and confidence which must subsist in the running of a 'quasi-partnership' company, which means a private company run like a partnership. The leading case, *Ebrahimi v Westbourne Galleries Ltd* (*1973*), involved the exclusion from management as one of the director/shareholders. We are not told that Fred is a director, but similar principles might apply to him, depending on the nature and mode of conduct of the company's affairs. Alternative relief could include an order for Anthony and Charles (or indeed the company itself) to purchase Fred's shares.

S. 75 CA 1980 severs (in a repeal and replacement of *s. 210*) the 'oppression' remedy from the winding up remedy so that it may be sought independently. It will no longer be necessary to show that the company could be wound up before the court can give alternative relief. Also, an isolated act will be sufficient rather than (as previously) a course of conduct. The new section refers to 'any actual or proposed act or omission' which is 'unfairly prejudicial' to some part of the members including the petitioner. *S. 75* might well make it easier for Fred to claim relief: it remains to be seen how the courts will interpret the section.

(iii) In *North-West Transportation Co Ltd v Beatty* (*1887*) it was held that a director who sold his boat to his company (in the absence of any fraud or oppression) could use his votes to ratify the transaction when the company voted on the issue in general meeting. Thus, the principle of majority rule usually means that majority shareholders may exercise their votes as they wish and the minority cannot complain. In *Clemens v Clemens Bros Ltd* (*1976*), however, the use, in circumstances similar to those contained in the question, of majority voting power by an aunt to the detriment of her niece was disallowed. The court held that the voting power must not be used unjustly. The decision has attracted adverse comment and there is doubt as to how far it will be applied in future cases. The same point would now be covered by the wide discretion now given to the courts to relieve oppression of minority shareholders by *s. 75 CA 1980* as indicated in (ii) above.

Fred should be advised accordingly.

ANSWER C1

(a) A director owes to his company a duty of disinterested exercise of his functions as director. He may not contract with or be interested in a contract with his company, even if the terms are fair to the company, unless the company has by its articles of association or by approval given in general meeting after full disclosure approved his conduct:

Aberdeen Railway v Blaikie Bros (*1854*). If the contract has been sanctioned, e.g. under an article like *Article 84*(*3*) of *Table A*, James may perhaps retain his profit unless other grounds exist for making him accountable.

If the value of copper rod is substantial, i.e. over £50,000 or 10% of the company's net assets but not less than £1,000 ('substantial property transaction'), the company may not enter into the arrangement unless it is *first* approved by a resolution of the company in general meeting. Thus, disclosure to the board would not satisfy this requirement: *s. 48 CA 1980*. If a company acts in breach of this provision the transaction is voidable at its option. In addition any director or person connected with a director who acted in contravention of the provision or authorised the transaction is liable to account to the company for any gain made and is liable to indemnify the company for any loss resulting from the transaction: *s. 48 CA 1980*.

These provisions are a substantial improvement on the previous confused situation. It is remarkable that the other directors were so ill-informed as to the market price. Was there collusion between them and James to defraud the company? Was James appointed agent with sole authority to purchase copper rod for the company? Are the directors controlling shareholders whose negligence in enriching a fellow director may be treated as equivalent to fraud (*Daniels v Daniels* (*1978*)? In such cases the company might be able to recover the difference between market price and contract price from the directors or James alone as damages for fraud. If James failed to disclose to the board the nature of his interest in the contract under *s. 199 CA 1948* he loses the benefit of provision of the articles permitting him to contract with the company. The company could then rescind the contract if it wished but it could not affirm the contract and claim the profit unless James had originally bought the goods on the company's behalf.

(b) Unless the articles of association otherwise provide, James, as an interested party, may not be counted in the necessary quorum at the board meeting nor may his vote be counted. There must be a disinterested majority. *Article 84*(*2*) of *Table A*, which gives some remissions, does not apply to a contract under which a director acts as vendor of his own property to the company.

ANSWER C2

For the transaction to be binding on the company, the company secretary must have been acting within his authority. It has been held that a company secretary may be assumed to have authority as agent of the company to make routine administrative contracts such as employing staff or ordering hire cars for company use: *Panorama Developments* (*Guildford*) *Ltd v Fidelis Furnishing Fabrics Ltd* (*1971*). Harry's past transactions are within these limits and so no question arises of any extension of his authority by holding out. In ordering a computer Harry has probably exceeded his implied authority as defined in the *Panorama Case*. A purchase of this size, even if of an 'administrative' item like a computer, is hardly routine or day-to-day in nature.

It would be open to the supplier to produce evidence, if he could, that it was normal practice for a secretary of a company of this type and size to make a contract for such an expensive and exceptional item. It seems unlikely that this could be established. A company secretary by virtue of his office has no inherent authority to make contracts except as stated.

ANSWER C3

As a general rule, using inside information to purchase shares from shareholders who lacked that information is not in breach of any director's duty to the vendors: *Percival v Wright (1902)*. Directors owe their duties to the company. They could only be liable if (which is not the case here) they had undertaken to act as agents of their shareholders in a re-sale: *Allen v Hyatt (1945)*. *CA 1980* introduced long awaited provisions covering *insider dealing*—i.e. the use of unpublished price-sensitive information to make a profit or avoid a loss. *S. 68 CA 1980* prohibits any individual who is knowingly connected with a company from dealing on a recognised stock exchange in securities in the company in which he has *inside* information. Getrich is a public quoted company so presumably the directors purchase shares on the stock market. In doing so it seems they are in breach of *s. 68 CA 1980*. Unfortunately, *s. 68* merely creates a criminal penalty and provides no compensation for the injured parties—i.e. those who sold out to the directors who would not have done so if they had had the same information as the directors.

Although the vendors of the shares have no remedies against the directors the company may be able to recover their profit as a benefit obtained (though not at the company's expense) from their office of directors. Every director owes a fiduciary duty to his company not to make a secret profit and not to use his powers for a collateral purpose. The directors are in breach of both these duties and are thus liable to account to the company for the breach: *Regal (Hastings) Ltd v Gulliver (1942)*.

ANSWER C4

(a) A person dealing with the directors of a company is deemed to be aware of any limits on their powers contained in the memorandum and articles of association but (in the absence of knowledge, actual or constructive, of facts to the contrary) may assume that any internal procedure by which the directors could have been given the necessary authority has been duly observed and carried through: *Royal British Bank v Turquand (1856)*. The rule does not however cover the acts of a *single director* merely because he could have been given delegated authority by the board: *Houghton & Co v Nothard Lowe & Wills Ltd (1927)*.

(b) If the outside traders wish to make Ribble Ltd liable on the contracts made between themselves and Harry, they must show that Harry has the authority of the company to enter into such contracts and that the company has the capacity to do so.

A director will have authority to enter into contracts as agent of the company if he is acting within his actual, implied or apparent authority. The outsiders can only rely on his having actual authority if there is an express provision to that effect in the public documents, but they could not rely merely on a power to delegate having been exercised in his favour: *Freeman and Lockyer v Buckhurst Park Properties Ltd* (*1964*). If the outsiders are attempting to rely on implied authority of directors it should be noted that such authority is very limited. *S. 9*(*1*) *ECA 1972* and the rule in *Turquand's Case* do not extend the authority of a director who acts on his own. The outsiders may show the company held Harry out as a person having authority to enter into such contracts, e.g. by acquiescing in previous, similar transactions.

If Harry is acting within his authority then unless the contracts are *ultra vires* they will be binding on the company. If the contracts are within Harry's authority and *ultra vires* they may still be binding on Ribble Ltd if the outsiders can rely on *s. 9*(*1*) *ECA 1972*—i.e. as long as they act in good faith and the transaction is decided on by the directors, third parties are not to be affected by any restrictions on the company's capacity to enter into contracts. It has been argued that a transaction entered into by one director is not one 'decided on by the *directors*' but this argument might be overcome by claiming that the directors, by holding Harry out, had decided on those contracts.

Finally, if the outsiders had inspected the memorandum and articles it would be difficult for them to assert that they are acting in good faith. However, as the burden of proof is on the company to show lack of good faith and the outsiders could always allege that they did not understand the memorandum and articles, and were, therefore, still acting in good faith, *s. 9* may still be of some value.

ANSWER C5

(a) The company and not an individual member of it is the proper plaintiff in an action to enforce the company's rights: *Foss v Harbottle* (*1843*). Under the articles of association (*Article 80 Table A*) the directors have the power to institute proceedings and there is nothing to suggest that they have not exercised that power in good faith in what they consider to be the company's interests. The company in general meeting cannot override the directors' decision not to sue by instructing them how they should exercise their powers: *Shaw & Sons Ltd v Shaw* (*1935*). But if the directors cannot or will not exercise their powers the company in general meeting may in some limited circumstances have a concurrent power to take a decision on the company's behalf. One such exceptional case is a failure (or inability) of the directors to institute legal proceedings on the company's behalf. Gower, in a passage approved by the House of Lords (*Alexander Ward & Co Ltd v Samyang Navigation Co Ltd* (*1975*)) argues that a decision to sue taken in general meeting is only effective in special cases where the directors have not *validly exercised* their powers because they are unable or unwilling to do so. Such situations arise where there are no directors (*Alexander Ward Case*) or where there is deadlock (*Barron v Potter* (*1914*)) or where a majority of the directors have an interest in preventing the institution of legal proceedings: *Marshall's Valve Gear Ltd v Manning Wardle & Co Ltd* (*1909*). Whether Henry can act on the authority of the general meeting depends on the circumstances of and reasons for the directors' failure to bring proceedings, i.e. the power to override them is much restricted.

(b) This appears to be a case of fraud on a company by its controlling shareholders for which a minority shareholder can bring proceedings on behalf of the company despite the passing of a resolution in general meeting to approve what has been done: *Cook v Deeks* (*1916*). Even if actual fraud by the directors cannot be established they have used their powers to transfer to themselves property of the company and so they are accountable: *Daniels v Daniels* (*1978*). Profits of a contract which the company could and would otherwise have secured are to be treated in equity as its property: *Cook v Deeks supra*. The directors can use their votes as members to pass a resolution in general meeting to approve a transaction in which they have an interest: *North-West Transportation Co Ltd v Beatty* (*1887*). But such approval is not effective in cases of fraud. It is likely (the question does not say so) that the directors hold a majority of votes since other shareholders would be unlikely to vote with them after disclosure of their conduct. It is uncertain whether a majority decision can be challenged if the directors' votes taken by themselves are only a minority. In the only case (*Atwool v Merryweather* (*1867*), the directors' votes, although a minority, were sufficient to swing the result in their own favour. But they had obtained shares (and votes) by fraud and had not made a full disclosure. Their votes were disqualified and the approval given was thus rescinded. In *Prudential Assurance Co Ltd v Newman Industries Ltd* (*1979*) the court held that factual control by the wrongdoers was sufficient to invoke the exception of fraud on the minority, but this decision was reversed on appeal.

If Henry could bring an action for fraud on the minority it would have to be in representative capacity for the company—i.e. a derivative action. Such an action if successful would in reality be the company's own action and any proceeds of the action would belong to the company not Henry.

ANSWER C6

A company may remove any directors from office by passing an ordinary resolution of which special notice has been given: *s. 184 CA 1948*. There is little advantage to A in the special notice procedure since there are no uncommitted shareholders to whom he can appeal. But B and C cannot remove him from his directorship at a *board* meeting as they threaten to do. They will have to use their power as a majority of the board to convene a general meeting and follow the special notice procedure under *s. 142 CA 1948*.

A could petition the court for a compulsory winding up order on the just and equitable ground: *s. 222(f) CA 1948*. It appears that as in *Ebrahimi v Westbourne Galleries Ltd* (*1973*) and *Re A & BC Chewing Gum* (*1975*), it is the underlying basis of the relationship that each of the three shareholders is to participate in the management as director: those rights of A would be infringed if he were removed from his office of director. A would have to satisfy the court that he had a tangible interest in the liquidation proceedings—i.e. the company must be solvent: *Re Yenidje Tobacco Co Ltd* (*1916*).

If A does not wish to put the company into liquidation he could apply for some alternative remedy under *s. 75 CA 1980* such as an order requiring B and C to purchase his shares at a fair value. This was the remedy granted to a minority shareholder in *Scottish Co-operative Wholesale Society v Meyer* (*1959*) under *s. 210 CA 1948*, which is now replaced by *s. 75 CA 1980*, but the remedies available are not affected. A would have to show that the affairs of the company were being conducted in a manner unfairly prejudicial to the interests of some part of the members, including at least A. By analogy to cases decided on *s. 210 CA 1948*, it would appear that although the shareholders are only threatening to do something which is within their power, i.e. remove a director, it could still amount to unfairly prejudicial conduct. Unfairly prejudicial conduct is probably not limited to unconstitutional acts.

A shareholder petitioning under *s. 210 CA 1948* could only succeed if he was petitioning in his capacity as a member and not in any other capacity, e.g. as a director: *Ebrahimi v Westbourne Galleries Ltd* (*1973*). The unfairly prejudicial conduct complained of by Alfred affects his interests in his capacity as a director. Thus *s. 75 CA 1980* may similarly not be available to him.

Finally, he could probably bring a minority shareholder's derivative action against B and C if he can show that the company is being deprived by them of its property, i.e. that the contracts are to be regarded as within the reach of the company before being diverted: *Cook v Deeks* (*1916*). Such an action would only be of indirect benefit to A as its proceeds would belong to the company and A would really be in no better position unless he could secure payment for his interest in the company by a winding-up as discussed above. In a winding-up, the liquidator could claim a refund of any secret profit made by B and and C by way of a misfeasance summons under *s. 333 CA 1948*.

ANSWER C7

Wide powers are given to the directors by the articles of association (e.g. *Table A Article 80*) but these are to be used for the benefit of the company and not for any collateral purpose of the directors themselves. If the directors misuse their powers they may be required to account to the company for any profit obtained and the transaction may be rendered void but not so as to prejudice an innocent outsider who may rely on the rule in *Turquand's Case* or *s. 9(1) ECA 1972*.

Some new regulations have been introduced by *CA 1980* as a result of these abuses of the directors' powers to issue shares. *S. 14 CA 1980* provides that directors must have authority from the shareholders before issuing new shares and *s. 17 CA 1980* gives existing shareholders pre-emption rights. These provisions will restrict some of the freedom of the directors but both provisions are limited and there is provision for their exclusion.

In the issue of shares it is the duty of the directors to obtain for the company whatever premium over par value is possible. The only exception is the offer of shares to existing shareholders under a rights issue; here some reduction of the market price is allowed since the benefit accrues to existing members in proportion to their shareholdings. It is certainly an abuse of the directors' powers to issue shares at less than their market value in order to obtain a proportion of the profit on re-sale.

The directors would also be held accountable for their illicit profit and, since the allottees are parties to the fraud, the allotment would be void.

Secondly, it is an improper use of the directors' powers to allot shares so as to create votes to be used in their favour: *Hogg v Cramphorn Ltd (1966)*. The use of a directors' powers honestly but for an improper purpose can be validated by a resolution passed in general meeting (if the votes which they have created are not used). But a fraudulent use of the directors' powers, even if they are not controlling the shareholders, probably cannot be so approved: *Atwool v Merryweather (1867)*.

ANSWER C8

A company is a separate legal entity but it cannot physically act for itself—it must always act through agents, usually the board of directors.

The company may have held out the director as a member of its board, e.g. by showing his name as a director in the list on its letterhead. Secondly, the outsider may be able to rely on the rule in *Turquand's Case* and assume that a person who acts as a director has been duly appointed as such: *Mahony v East Holyford Mining Co (1875)*. Both principles only assist an outsider who does not know or suspect that the director has not been properly appointed.

Two statutory provisions may also assist him. The acts of a director are valid in spite of the subsequent discovery of an irregularity in his appointment or qualification: *s. 180 CA 1948*. But this rule does not apply where there has been no purported appointment at all or the director has ceased to hold office: *Morris v Kanssen (1946)*. Secondly, a company which fails to give notice to the Registrar of Companies of a change among its directors, such as a director ceasing to hold office, cannot rely on that fact (to repudiate the acts of the director) unless the other party with whom the director deals is aware of the true position: *s. 9(4) ECA 1972*.

For these reasons it is usually not necessary for a person dealing with an apparent company director to check that he has been appointed (and still is) a director of the company which he represents. But a single director (other than a managing director) is not by virtue of his office alone an agent authorised to make contracts on behalf of the company, so it may be necessary to obtain confirmation that he is so authorised—and thus incidentally that he is a director. Unlike a partner of a firm who has the apparent authority of his firm to act as an agent, a single director has little or no such apparent authority.

ANSWER C9

The holders of at least 10% of the voting shares of a company may (*s. 132 CA 1948*) require the directors to call a general meeting. This is done by depositing at the registered office a requisition signed by the shareholders and stating the purpose for which the meeting is to be called. The directors must within three weeks of the deposit of the requisition call a meeting. If the directors do not convene the meeting the requisitionists, or a majority of them, may convene the meeting themselves for a date within three months of the deposit of the requisition. Their expenses are paid by the company and deducted from sums payable by the company to the directors.

As the purpose of the meeting is to remove the directors from office the requisitionists would also, in depositing their requisition, give special notice (*s. 142 CA 1948*) of their intention. This is notice to the company given 28 days before the meeting. The notice of the meeting would set out the resolution for removal of the directors. The directors themselves are entitled to receive a copy of the special notice from the company; to circulate 'representations' in their defence to members; and to be heard at the meeting itself.

Any members may under this procedure (*s. 184 CA 1948*) propose the removal of directors, but, unless there is some special provision in the memorandum and articles to the contrary, the directors can refuse to include the resolution in the notice covering the meeting unless the requisitionist(s) can muster at least half of the voting rights or a hundred or more members holding at least £100 on average of the nominal share capital: *Pedley v Inland Waterways Association Ltd* (*1977*). The resolution itself will be passed only if a majority of votes is cast in its favour at the meeting. The shareholders' committee must therefore have or obtain a majority of votes cast for their resolution.

Since no Annual General Meeting has been held for almost two years, the shareholders' committee could as an alternative procedure apply to the Department of Trade under *s. 131 CA 1948* for an order that an Annual General Meeting be held. This might suit them if they lack the 10% support required for a *s. 132* procedure but reckon to attract sufficient support when the meeting is convened to carry a resolution under *s. 184 CA 1948*.

ANSWER C10

(a) The office of a director is gratuitous; he is not permitted to make a profit from his appointment without consent by the shareholders.

Payment to a director of compensation for loss of office may only be made after disclosure to the members of the company of the proposed payment and its approval in general meeting: *s. 191 CA 1948*. The same rule is extended by *s. 192 CA 1948* to any payment of compensation or as consideration for retirement from office in connection with the sale of the company's undertaking and property or any part of it. In this case disclosure and approval is required even if the payment is to be made by an outsider, e.g. the purchaser and not by the company itself. If a director receives compensation without complying with *s. 192* he holds the sum received in trust for the company. The same principle also applies when a bid is made for a company's shares and compensation is to be paid to the directors: *s. 193*. In such a case, if a director fails to disclose the proposed payment and to obtain approval, he holds the compensation on trust for any persons who sold their shares as a result of the bid.

Accordingly any compensation to be paid to John and Harry for loss of their offices as directors must be disclosed to members and approved in general meeting. This is so, whichever of the two methods mentioned in the question is used and whether the compensation is to be paid by the company (*s. 191*) or by the purchaser: *ss. 192 and 193*.

However, John also has a service agreement with five years to run. If the company terminates this agreement before its expiry date the company becomes liable to pay damages for breach of contract: *Southern Foundries (1926) Ltd v Shirlaw (1940)*. Such damages are explicitly excluded (by *s. 194*) from the rules of *ss. 191–193*.

CA 1980 provides that a contract of employment of a director with no or limited provision for termination by the company cannot exceed five years unless the term (regarding length of service) is first approved by a resolution of the shareholders. If this has not occurred in John's case the term would be void, and a term providing that the contract could be terminated on giving reasonable notice would be implied instead: *s. 47 CA 1980*. John could only claim damages for failure to give reasonable notice. This rule applies to contracts made on or after 22nd December 1980.

(b) Whichever method of acquisition is adopted there must be a circular sent to all members of the company (even if not entitled to attend and vote) setting out the amount and other particulars of the compensation for loss of office proposed in each case. The proposal must be approved by the members in general meeting.

Under *s. 194* these rules apply to any compensation paid within one year before or two years after the sale or take-over, and compensation includes any indirect payment such as a higher price for directors' shares than is paid for others.

ANSWER C11

Although a company is a separate legal entity, distinct from its members and managers, the courts will lift this veil of incorporation in some cases, especially if there is evidence of fraud. Under *s. 332 CA 1948*, if on a winding up it appears that the business of the company has been carried on with intent to defraud creditors, the court may order that the persons who were knowingly parties to the carrying on of business in this way shall be personally liable for all or any of the company's debts or liabilities, if the court so orders. It is also a criminal offence.

In *Re William C Leitch Bros Ltd* (*1932*) it was said that if a company continues to carry on business and to incur debts without any *reasonable* prospect that those debts will be paid, it is in general a proper inference that the business is being carried on with intent to defraud. But although dishonest intention may be inferred some evidence, even if indirect, of dishonesty is necessary: *Re Patrick & Lyon Ltd* (*1933*). Only those persons who join in a decision to continue trading in these circumstances, i.e. the directors, and anyone else who *actively participates*, can be *parties* to the decision: *Re Maidstone Building Provisions Ltd* (*1971*).

Mere intent to prefer one creditor over another where a person knew or had reason to believe that he would have insufficient assets to pay all creditors in full could not constitute 'fraudulent' trading within *s. 332: Re Sarflax* (*1979*).

The fact that the company continues to trade in such circumstances is not therefore *conclusive* evidence of intent to defraud but places on the directors and any other person involved the burden of showing that there were reasonable grounds for believing that debts would be paid.

It all therefore depends on whether the directors' optimism about the future is mere wishful thinking or hoping 'something will turn up' or whether they can foresee a probable return to profitability, e.g. as a result of reducing costs or raising prices or putting a new product on the market.

The directors would do well to prepare a written assessment of the prospects of recovery and solvency as they see it to justify their optimism. It would be sensible to bring in the company's auditors as independent experts to assist them in their analysis and forecast.

ANSWER C12

(i) As a shareholder Smith is entitled to attend the meeting and to speak at it. The ordinary business of an Annual General Meeting includes a resolution for the adoption of the accounts. In moving that resolution the chairman is likely (in accordance with modern practice) to invite questions on the financial affairs of the company from shareholders present. But if he does not follow that practice Smith can address the meeting expressing his views on the directors' policy and putting his questions. However, the directors are under no obligation to answer his questions though it would be a sign of weakness for them flatly to refuse to do so.

(ii) The resolution which Smith wishes to propose would be special business (ordinary business is defined by *Article 52* of *Table A* and anything else is special). Notice of Smith's resolution would have to be given in the notice convening the meeting. If the directors refuse to include this item in the notice to be issued to shareholders Smith can only compel them to do so if he and his supporters (if any) hold at least 5% of the shares carrying voting rights or if they number at least 100 members holding shares on which at least £100 (average per member) has been paid up: *s. 140 CA 1948*. If the resolution is not included in the notice Smith cannot move it: *Pedley v Inland Waterways Association* (*1977*). He could however oppose the directors' resolution for the adoption of the accounts as an implied vote of censure.

Even if Smith can secure the inclusion of his resolution in the notice and carry it at the meeting it will be of no legal effect insofar as it seeks to instruct the directors how they should exercise powers of management entrusted to them by the articles (*Article 80* of *Table A*): *Quin & Axtens Ltd v Salmon* (*1909*).

(iii) There are no special rules applicable to voting against the re-election of directors who have retired by rotation. This is not a case of removal from office before the expiration of the period of office under *s. 184 CA 1948*. The directors will have retired under the articles (*Article 90* of *Table A*); any member present can vote against their re-election if he wishes. But if he wished to propose that he himself or some other alternative candidate should be elected a director in place of a retiring director whose re-election was recommended by the board, Smith would under the articles (*Article 93* of *Table A*) have to give notice to the company (with the signed consent of his candidate) not less than three days or more than 21 before the meeting.

If more than one director is standing for election or re-election each must be voted on individually unless the meeting resolves without a dissentient to vote on them collectively: *s. 183 CA 1948*. This rule applies only to public companies.

ANSWER C13

Subject to any overriding provisions of the Companies Acts and of the memorandum of association, a company may by special resolution alter its articles of association.

There are a number of limiting principles, both of the Companies Acts and of case law, but the only rule which is relevant to the facts of the question is that a company cannot be prevented from altering its articles because in doing so it commits or facilitates the breach of a separate contract: *Southern Foundries* (*1926*) *Ltd v Shirlaw* (*1940*); *Shindler v Northern Raincoat Co Ltd* (*1960*). These cases also establish that when a company applies its articles, with or without alteration, so as to breach such a contract, the other party may claim damages for the breach. The facts given in the question have some points in common with those of *Shirlaw's Case*, but there are also significant differences.

In *Shirlaw's Case*, as in the facts of the question, the service agreement is a contract distinct from the articles of association, but it is also connected with the articles because the working director cannot serve the company as such if he is deprived of his directorship under the articles.

The facts of the question, however, differ from those of *Shirlaw's Case* in that J has not lost his directorship by the unilateral act of the company in altering the articles. The company has imposed on every director a new requirement, i.e. the acquisition of qualification shares, by a valid procedure which J cannot restrain. J then has the choice of either compliance with the new articles (it is assumed that it is possible for him to acquire the shares which are needed) or of failing to do so. He has elected not to comply and so the termination of his directorship, and the incidental breach of his service agreement, is his act and not the company's.

Two further issues then arise. First, the company has in effect inserted into the service agreement a new condition for holding a directorship. Is the company free to do so? Secondly, did J cease to be a director as soon as the new article was brought into effect or at some later time, and if so when? Both points were considered in *Molineaux v London Birmingham and Manchester Insurance Co* (*1902*), where the facts were similar except that the provision of the articles dealing with an existing directors' qualifying shareholding was altered to increase the required shareholding from 50 to 250 shares and the alteration was made as a preliminary to the publication of a prospectus. In *Molineaux's Case* it was held that what is now *s. 182 CA 1948* has no application to such facts: *s. 182 CA 1948* merely disqualifies a director, if, following his appointment, he fails within two months to acquire qualification shares or at any time ceases to hold them. The imposition of a new qualification requirement on a director already in office at the time is a different situation for which *s. 182 CA 1948* does not provide. The company is free to impose this new condition on the director through the alteration of its articles, but he has a reasonable period of time in which to comply with it if he elects to continue as director. In *Molineaux's Case* it was held that he should have acquired the additional shares before the publication of the prospectus. In J's case the relevant circumstances would determine what was a reasonable period; for example it might be the time in which he could have had shares transferred into his name if he had set out to do so.

For these reasons J has no valid claim against the company.

ANSWER C14

Burnaby's claim against the company is enforceable only if the contracts for his design work were contracts binding on the company. Two issues are involved: did the company act within its capacity and did the director act within his authority?

The company's principal object is to carry on the business of house-builders and it also has express power (the power would be implied even if it had not been expressly given) to enter into transactions incidental to that object. Contracts for design work by an architect are incidental to the building work for which the designs are required. Accordingly the contracts with Burnaby were within the capacity of, i.e. *intra vires*, the company: *Attorney General v Great Eastern Railway* (*1880*).

The next issue is whether the company, having the power to do so, did in fact make binding contracts for Burnaby's services. A company can only make a contract through an authorised agent since the company itself is an abstract person. The articles, which are in the form of *Table A*, provide in *Article 80* that all powers of management are vested in the board of directors on behalf of the company subject to limitations which do not apply in this case.

Burnaby however has been dealing with a single director (Wright). The board of directors may have delegated to Wright their powers of making these contracts (*Table A Article 102*). In this case Burnaby can only rely on Wright having authority to contract on behalf of the company if he can prove that the directors' power of delegation was exercised in Wright's favour. Alternatively, the board may have appointed Wright as managing director (*Table A Article 107*) with appropriate powers. In such a case contracts with Burnaby made by Wright would be binding on the company.

ANSWER C15

The article that is cited is to be found in the model *Table A Article 80* provision, which has been the subject of considerable litigation. Where there is such provision the basic principle is that the ultimate repository of authority is the board of directors of the company. The general meeting of the company is not in a position to instruct the board of directors as to how the affairs of the company should be conducted.

This principle does give way to certain exceptions. For example, the general meeting can resolve to take legal action where the board omits to do so (*Marshall's Valve Gear Ltd v Manning Wardle & Co Ltd* (*1909*)), and the articles may not be overridden by the board of directors. However, it does not appear that this case falls within the exceptional categories.

Other courses of action are open to the disenchanted shareholders. First, they would be well advised to ensure that the activity of manufacturing car batteries is in fact *intra vires*, though there is no circumstance to indicate otherwise on the facts stated.

Secondly, a majority is in a position to dismiss directors by ordinary resolution under *s. 184 CA 1948* notwithstanding anything that the articles or memorandum may say to the contrary. The threat of such a resolution may secure the compliance of the directors.

Thirdly, the articles and therefore the directors' powers could be altered for the future (assuming the necessary majority can be obtained): *s. 10 CA 1948*. However, this could not alter the present position.

In addition to the question of the control within a company, the problem raises the question of directors' duties. Until recently directors only owed duties to the providers of capital, i.e. the shareholders, and owed no duty to take into account the interests of the providers of labour, i.e. employees.

S. 46 CA 1980 now provides that 'The matters to which the directors of a company are to have regard in the performance of their functions shall include the interests of the company's employees in general as well as the interests of its members.'

This means that an action may be maintained for failure to take proper account of the interests of the company's employees, but an action can only be brought by a shareholder: *s. 46(2) CA 1980.*

ANSWER C16

This company is a private limited company. Under the principle in *Salomon v Salomon & Co Ltd (1897)* a company is in law a separate person from its members. If the company has, as in this case, been formed with limited liability and its shares are fully paid, its members will normally have no liability for its debts. Exceptions to this principle (*lifting the veil of incorporation*) include (1) a company whose membership is reduced below the statutory minimum, and (2) a company which in liquidation is found to have carried on business with intent to defraud creditors.

When Mac and Sheena die their shares pass by operation of law to their personal representatives; Mac and Sheena cease to be members for the purposes of *s. 31 CA 1948*, nor do their personal representatives become members automatically. Some companies' articles permit personal representatives to register themselves as members but it is more likely that the person entitled to Mac and Sheena's shares under their wills or on intestacy will eventually become members. Ewan could try and hurry up either process.

S. 31 CA 1948 as amended by *CA 1980* provides that if (1) the membership of a company is reduced below the statutory minimum (two) and (2) the company continues to carry on business for the six months in this situation, then (3) any member who is aware of these facts becomes liable without limit for the debts of the company incurred in its business after the end of the six months' period. Ewan would therefore become liable for the company's debts if he allows the existing situation to continue for a further three months. But he can avoid this by transferring some of his own shares to a nominee who would (with Ewan himself) make up the required minimum of two members. As Ewan is the sole surviving director he may well have to co-opt his nominee on to the board to make up a quorum to approve the transfer (*Table A Articles 99, 100 and 95*). Alternatively, he could petition the court for a winding up order: *s. 222 CA 1948.*

S. 332 CA 1948 applies when a company is in liquidation and provides that any person who has knowingly carried on the business of the company with intent to defraud creditors shall be liable for its debts (if the court so directs). If the company is already insolvent due to its heavy losses Ewan risks liability under *s. 332* in a subsequent liquidation unless he can show that there are reasonable grounds for believing that the debts incurred will be paid: *Re William C Leitch Bros Ltd* (*1932*). He should take stock of the existing financial situation and prospects of future trading at a profit and decide whether such grounds exist.

ANSWER C17

In *Re City Equitable Fire Insurance Co Ltd* (*1925*) a company had lost £1.2 million partly as a result of the dishonesty of the managing director. The liquidator sought to make the other directors liable on the grounds that their want of skill and care had given the opportunity for the fraud. In reviewing the general law three procedures were laid down.

First, a director is only required to exhibit in the performance of his duties that degree of *skill* which may reasonably be expected from a person of his particular knowledge and experience. A director of an insurance company is not required to have the skill of an actuary—unless of course he is one.

Secondly, a director as such is *not* required to give *continuous attention* to the affairs of the company. His duty is to attend meetings of the board and of any committees of the board of which he is a member. If of course he is also an employee his duties *in that capacity* will probably require him to devote the whole of his working time to the company.

Thirdly, in the absence of grounds of suspicion, he is entitled to *trust* employees of the company to whom responsibilities have been properly delegated. If a company cheque is presented to him for signature he should be aware of the purpose for which it is drawn but he need not investigate the whole matter himself. He should see that the company's surplus moneys are properly invested but need not ascertain where the share certificates have been deposited.

ANSWER C18

These terms have been introduced by *CA 1980* in connection with directors' duties. Quasi-loans and connected persons are relevant to the prohibitions on loans to directors by companies and shadow directors are relevant generally to the statutory duties imposed on directors. They are all necessary anti-avoidance provisions.

(a) A quasi-loan. This is defined in *s. 65 CA 1980* as a transaction under which one party (the creditor) agrees to pay or does pay a sum for another (the borrower) or agrees to reimburse or does reimburse expenditure incurred by another party, or the circumstances give rise to a liability on the borrower to reimburse the creditor.

S. 49 CA 1980 prohibits companies making loans to their directors except in very limited circumstances (this provision replaces *s. 190 CA 1948*, which had a number of defects). A company is similarly prohibited from making quasi-loans, as defined above, to its directors as otherwise the methods outlined in *s. 65* would constitute easy ways of avoiding *s. 49 CA 1980.*

Creditor (the company)
liable to reimburse / \ payment of a sum or reimbursement of expenses
Director (........X (a non-director))
some 'arrangement'

(b) A connected person, *S. 64 CA 1980* defines a connected person as any person who is the director's spouse, child or step-child; any company with which the director is associated; a person acting in his capacity as trustee under an employee's share scheme, the beneficiaries of which include the director, his spouse and/or children; a partner of the director; or of any of the above connected persons. The prohibition on loans to directors by public companies extends to loans and quasi-loans to connected persons as defined in *s. 64*. This plugs one of the gaps in the old *s. 190 CA 1948* prohibition.

(c) A shadow director. This is a person in accordance with whose directions or instructions the directors of a company are accustomed to act. Any such person is treated as a director for the purposes of *Part IV CA 1980*—i.e. duties of directors and conflicts of interest. Thus, a person cannot avoid the liability of being a director where he acts as a director or managing director but is not appointed as such. Where the directors only act on another's directions and instructions given by that person in a professional capacity, that person will not be a shadow director. This covers solicitors, accountants, etc. advising company directors on professional matters: *s. 63 CA 1980.*

ANSWER C19

S. 142 CA 1948 provides that the resolution of which special notice has been given shall be included in the notice to members convening a general meeting to consider it. But the directors are not obliged to do this unless the special notice is given by members holding at least 5% of the voting shares or at least 100 members as required by *s. 140 CA 1948: Pedley v Inland Waterways Association Ltd* (*1977*). If the resolution is accepted for consideration at a general meeting Harold is entitled to be given a copy of it at once since he may be removed from office at the meeting by an ordinary resolution: *s. 184 CA 1948.*

Harold may by *s. 184* explain his case to members of the company in two ways. He is entitled to make written representations of reasonable length which the company should issue with the notice of the meeting; or if received too late they must be read at the meeting. Secondly, Harold may address the meeting. He should avoid giving Peter grounds for an action for defamation or for application to the court (under *s. 184*) for an order restraining needless publicity of defamatory matter.

If Harold is removed from his directorship he is still entitled to damages for breach of his service agreement: *s. 184(6) CA 1948*.

The particular clause in Harold's contract is one which requires prior approval by a resolution of the company in general meeting under *s. 47 CA 1980*. If no approval has been obtained for the inclusions of this clause, then the original agreement is deemed to include a term entitling the company to terminate it at any time on giving reasonable notice. Any damages for breach of contract would have to be adjusted accordingly. However, *s. 47* applies only to agreements entered into on or after 22 Dec. 1980.

Harold may possibly be able to counter-attack by persuading the board of directors or the company in general meeting that proceedings should be begun against Peter to recover the money which he has misappropriated. If Peter is the controlling shareholder, Harold (if he is himself a shareholder) can bring proceedings himself on behalf of the company as an exception to the rule in *Foss v Harbottle* (*1843*); *Cook v Deeks* (*1916*); *Wallersteiner v Moir* (*1975*).

If Harold and Peter are members of a small number of shareholders in a personal relationship, Harold might also be able to petition for the winding up of the company: *Re Westbourne Galleries* (*1973*). Probably, Harold could not use the 'unfairly prejudicial conduct' provisions of *s. 75 CA 1980* because these are for the benefit of members who are being prejudiced as such and removal from the directorship does not affect membership.

ANSWER C20

CA 1980 Part V made insider dealing a criminal offence for the first time. The maximum penalty is two years' imprisonment and/or a fine of £1,000.

It is assumed that the sale by Herbert was a sale on the stock exchange: the legislation is confined to the shares of public listed companies and to stock exchange or off-market deals or investment exchange deals in such securities. If there was no such deal, Herbert has committed no offence.

The basis of the newly created offence is:

(a) *Prohibitions on an 'insider'*

An 'insider' is an individual who *is or has been within the past 6 months knowingly connected with a company:* 'connected' means a director, or an officer, employee or individual in a position involving a professional or business relationship who may reasonably be expected to have access to unpublished price-sensitive information. The individuals connected in a similar way with holding company subsidiary or fellow subsidiary companies are also caught by the definition. Clearly, professional advisers, including accountants and auditors, are included. A 'tippee' who *knowingly* obtained information is also covered by the Act.

(b) *Unpublished price-sensitive information*

Unpublished price-sensitive information must be specific and not merely of a general nature, not generally known to persons likely to deal in the securities and likely materially to affect the price if known. Clearly, unpublished information about risks or falls in profit (as in the question) is in this category.

(c) *What is prohibited?*

An insider who is knowingly in possession of unpublished price sensitive information about securities listed on a recognised stock exchange obtained by reason of his connection with the company and which it would be reasonable to expect him not to disclose except in the proper performance of his functions must not:

(1) deal in the securities,

(2) counsel or procure someone else to do so,

(3) communicate the information to another person if he has reasonable cause to believe that such person or some other person will make use of the information to deal, to counsel or procure or turn to 'tip' someone else to do so.

How do the parties fare on this basis? Arthur is clearly 'connected' because he is employed by the company's auditors. Sandra is probably not so connected because she is not likely because of her job to have access to unpublished, price-sensitive information. However, although Arthur does not deal he 'tips' Sandra and if he has reason to think her husband will deal, he commits the offence. Sandra is therefore what has become known as a 'tippee' and she too is prohibited from dealing or passing on the information to anyone likely to deal: she has committed the offence by in turn 'tipping' Herbert. If Herbert on the basis of the tip sold his shares on the stock exchange or through an investment exchange or otherwise off-market, he has committed the offence also, unless perhaps he sold merely to pay his debts and not with the motive of using the information to avoid a loss.

ANSWER C21

All contracts made by a company which are not authorised by its memorandum or are not incidental to the carrying out of its objects are void unless they are made enforceable by *s. 9 ECA 1972*. However, this is not necessarily the case where the contract is not patently *ultra vires*.

S. 9 ECA 1972 applies and may render an *ultra vires* contract enforceable by the other party to it where that other party deals with the company's board of directors, but the section does not apply where the contract is concluded, as here, with any other representative of the company.

Thus the national distributor (Distributor) should enquire as to the company's capacity to contract. He should inspect the memorandum, because if he does not he will be regarded as having constructive notice of it since he is not within the scope of *s. 9*, which abolishes the doctrine of constructive notice where the other party to the contract deals with the board of directors.

Of course, if the contract is not patently *ultra vires* then it will be enforceable. Thus, in *Re Jon Beauforte* (*London*) *Ltd* (*1953*) a person who supplied goods (in this case coke) to a company which was formed to make ladies clothing but in fact made veneered wall panels, was only disabled from suing for the value of the goods because the order for the coke was on headed paper describing the company as 'veneered wall panel manufacturers'. But for this the claim would have succeeded because an inspection of the memorandum, actually or constructively, would not have revealed that the goods were bought for an *ultra vires* purpose.

As regards the authority of Ernest, *s. 9*—which cures lack of authority in the directors where the other party deals with the board—does not apply here, because Distributor is not dealing with the board.

We must therefore refer to the general law, under which directors have no power to act individually as agents for the company; they must have actual authority from the board to act. This is however subject to the very important principle enunciated in *Royal British Bank v Turquand* (*1856*)—the so-called Indoor Management Rule—whereby it was held that so long as the act done in the company's name is consistent with the company's registered documents (memorandum, articles etc.) an outsider is not bound to inquire whether all the necessary steps have been taken: that is to say he is entitled to assume that the transaction is *intra vires* the officer's authority. In this respect it is significant that, with appointments of a managing director usually made by the board, a search at the Companies Registry will not normally reveal information as to the propriety or otherwise of an individual holding himself out in such an office.

Moreover, a managing director is invested with usual or apparent authority to carry on the company's business in the usual way and to do all acts and enter into all contracts necessary for that purpose, and this is so even if he has not been appointed as such, provided the board has expressly or (as seems the case here) impliedly held him out as having power to represent the company (*Freeman and Lockyer v Buckhurst Park Properties Ltd* (*1964*)).

This would not apply if the other party to the contract actually *knew* that the managing director did not have an authority. It should be noted however that cases such as *Freeman* do not allow a managing director to make binding contracts where these are *ultra vires* the company.

Thus, provided Distributor has no knowledge of Ernest's lack of authority (should this be the case), and provided there is nothing in the circumstances of the transaction which would make a reasonable man suspicious and put him on enquiry, Distributor can rely on the apparent authority of Ernest and need not make enquiry as to his authority. There is of course nothing to stop Distributor doing so; but the need is by no means so great as is the need to enquire as to the company's capacity.

ANSWER C22

The shareholder should be advised that the matter is covered by *s. 140 CA 1948*.

The section provides that a member or members representing not less than 1/20th of the total voting rights of all members, or 100 or more members holding shares in the company on which there has been paid up an average of not less than £100 per member, can by making a written requisition to the company compel the company through its directors:

(a) to give to members who are entitled to have notice of the next annual general meeting, notice of any resolution which may properly be moved and which it is intended will be moved at that meeting; and
(b) to circulate to members any statement of up to 1,000 words dealing with the resolution.

So basically it depends on whether the shareholder has the requisite 1/20th of the voting power, because, if he has not, the directors are quite within their rights in refusing to place the resolution regarding the company's head office on the agenda (*Pedley v Inland Waterways Association Ltd* (*1977*)). If the shareholder does not have the requisite shareholding he must seek the support of other shareholders until he has managed to satisfy either formula of *s. 140*.

If he can obtain this support the requisition must be signed by the requisitionists and deposited at the registered office of the company not less than six weeks before the meeting. This is because a resolution is required and notice must be given of it. The item ranks as special business.

The shareholder should also be advised that there will have to be tendered within the requisition a sum reasonably adequate to meeting the company's expenses in giving effect to the resolution, otherwise the company need not act on it. All expenses must be borne by the requisitionist(s) unless at the meeting the members otherwise resolve.

S. 140 does not apply if the intention is to secure needless publicity for defamatory or abusive matter; but this would not appear to be the case on the facts given.

The directors cannot defeat *s. 140* by calling the AGM less than six weeks after the deposit of the requisition. If they do, sub-section 4 provides that nevertheless the section is deemed complied with. Failure by the directors to put a properly requisitioned resolution on the agenda of the AGM can result in a criminal prosecution.

The shareholder in question should, however, be further advised that, even if he is successful in having his proposal placed on the agenda, it does not follow that its approval as a resolution by majority decision of the membership will have the impact he desires. If the articles of Goldplate Ltd follow, for example, *Article 80* of *Table A*—which is most probable—the business of managing the company will be delegated to the directors. The board would therefore be entitled to disregard the majority view expressed in general meeting (*Automatic Self-Cleansing Filter Syndicate Co Ltd v Cunninghame* (*1906*)) because, as long as the company's existing constitution continues, the resolution does not supersede the directors' authority (*Scott v Scott* (*1943*)). The shareholder would, in such an event, have to seek to change the board's composition or to amend the company's articles by special resolution.

Tutorial note

The 'division of powers', which ensures that shareholders cannot normally interfere with the manner in which the board chooses to exercise the powers delegated to it, will not, of course, prevent action against the directors if they are in breach of their fiduciary duties. They will be in breach if they do not exercise their powers for the purpose for which they were given, *bona fide* for the benefit of the company as a whole, or if they use their powers for their own selfish benefit.

ANSWER C23

It is a basic rule of company law that directors must exercise the powers conferred upon them *bona fide* in the interests of the company (*Re Smith and Fawcett Ltd* (*1942*)); and it is *prima facie* for the directors to decide what really is in the 'interests of the company'. Actions beyond the scope of the principle are, at common law, *ultra vires* and void.

The powers of the company derive from:

(i) express objects stated in the memorandum;
(ii) inherent powers granted by statute, such as the right to alter the articles (by special resolution); and
(iii) authority implied as being necessary, or reasonably or necessarily incidental, and for the benefit of the company. An example of an implied power is that to employ people and to pay wages, or even pensions; but it has been held, for example, that it would not be an implied power to pay gratuitous pensions to directors' widows, unless this be done for the company's benefit (*Re Lee Behrens & Co Ltd* (*1932*)).

The pre-1980 position as far as *employees* were concerned was that the promotion of their interests was only legitimate if it ultimately advanced the interests of the shareholders (*Hutton v West Cork Railway Co* (*1883*)). Now, *CA 1980* specifically lays down that the matters to which the directors of a company are to have regard shall include the interests of that company's employees in general, as well as the interests of its members (*s. 46*). However, such a duty is owed to the company as such and not to employees individually, the obligation being enforceable in the same manner as any other fiduciary duty. However, the lack of any mention in *s. 46* of an employee's right to enforce the new obligation attaches a degree of weakness and uncertainty to this widening of the scope of a board's duties.

A further impact of the 1980 legislation stems from its statutory reversal of *Parke v Daily News Ltd* (*1962*). In that case the defendant company professed to make gratuitous payments to its employees in the course of a winding up. As there would be no company to be a future employer this could not be a payment made for the 'interests of the company', and was held to be *ultra vires*. *S. 74* destroys this decision by enacting that the powers of a company shall be deemed to include authority to make provision for employees in the case of a cessation or transfer of business.

Such power may only be exercised if sanctioned

(a) by ordinary resolution of the company; or
(b) if so authorised by the memorandum or articles, by a resolution of the directors; or
(c) by whatever resolution is required by the memorandum or articles.

The liquidator on winding up has similar powers, provided the liabilities of the company have been met in full.

Thus the significance of *s. 46* is that it provides statutory recognition that the interests of the company include provision for employees, whilst *s. 74* goes further by laying down that such provision on a winding up or other cessation or transfer of business shall not be *ultra vires* even if not capable of benefiting the company.

Both additions to company law have been widely welcomed as granting recognition of the employee group, and accord with the recommendations of the 1977 Bullock Committee of Inquiry on industrial democracy. Participation by employees in the management of companies is an area which will need legislation in due course to implement the EEC Fifth Directive on Company Law once this has been adopted.

ANSWER C24

(a) *Liability of the directors—s. 332 CA 1948*

The above statutory provision comprises both criminal and civil liability where, in the course of a winding up, it appears that directors have been responsible for fraudulent trading. The criminal liability will not be considered further; but if the directors of J and J Ltd have the intention to defraud they could be so liable.

As far as civil liability is concerned the general rule is that the company is liable for its own debts, with the directors as agents incurring no personal liability. *S. 332* qualifies this by laying down that if in the case of a winding up it appears that any business of the company has been carried on with intent to defraud creditors, or for any fraudulent purpose, the court, on application by the Official Receiver or the liquidator, a creditor or contributory, may declare that any persons who were knowingly parties to the carrying on of the business in that matter shall be personally responsible for all or any of the debts of the company. Thus it is possible that John and his wife could be liable for J and J Ltd's debts if they continue to trade in the corporate name knowing that the company is insolvent.

Case law in the interpretation of the section is not abundant. However, in *Re Maidstone Building Provisions Ltd* (*1971*) it was held that the expression 'party to' means participates in, takes part in or concurs in. It is thus possible that Jill would not be responsible under the section, as she takes no active part in the business.

More difficulty attaches to the concept of being 'knowingly' a party to the fraudulent carrying on of the undertaking. John is the managing director and must of necessity take an active part in the business. In *Re William C Leitch Bros Ltd* (*1932*) it was held that it would be a proper inference to deduce an intent to defraud if the company continues to carry on business and to incur debts at a time when there is to the knowledge of the directors no reasonable prospect of the creditors receiving payment of those debts.

Thus, it is not necessary for John to have criminal intent as such; mere knowledge would suffice. However, proceedings under the section are rare, since it is difficult to prove 'knowledge'. Directors may be optimistic about the future, and they may see light at the end of the tunnel. (For this reason the Cork Committee on insolvency considered alternatives such as 'wrongful trading', where the onus of proof would be less difficult.) John may therefore seek to claim that, although he is aware of present insolvency, he honestly believes that the situation is only a temporary one. Although there are dicta—by Maugham J in *Leitch* and by Buckley J in *Re White and Osmond* (*Parkstone*) *Ltd* (*1960*)—that suggest that such a *bona fide* belief can sometimes fend off a *s. 332* claim, it does also appear that such a belief must be reasonably based. In the present case John has received expert advice that the company appears to be insolvent, with no qualification as to likely future revival. Any subsequently incurred debts could in such circumstances well amount to being fraudulent, as even a single transaction could then properly be described as a fraud on the creditor (*Re Gerald Cooper Chemicals Ltd* (*1978*)).

(b) *Proof of insolvency*

It is necessary to prove that the present contingent and prospective debts of the company exceed the present value of its assets (*Re Capital Annuities Ltd* (*1979*)).

For this purpose the paid up value of the capital is not a debt. Thus it will be necessary to show that if the company ceased business it could meet its liabilities in full from the realisation of its assets. This would require a full list of the liabilities and assets together with material contracts and arrangements for the provision of finance by bankers etc. This would be similar to the declaration of solvency to be filed prior to a members' voluntary winding up, i.e. a statement that there has been a review of the debts and in the opinion of the directors they can be met in full within a period not exceeding 12 months.

The only escape route from the inability to provide such present solvency might lie in a persuasion of the accountant that profitable future activities were a practicable possibility or that the shareholders were genuinely prepared to inject fresh capital into the ailing company. Very firm evidence would be needed to attract a professional accountant to this conclusion.

Tutorial note

Under *CA 1981*, the *criminal* (but not civil) aspects of *s. 332 CA 1948* are extended to cover participating in fraudulent trading even if there is no liquidation. Thus criminal prosecution can result whether or not the company is wound up.

ANSWER C25

(a) An auditor, although properly qualified and a member of a recognised professional accountancy body, is nevertheless disqualified from acting as auditor by *s. 161 CA 1948* as a result of certain relationships. A person cannot be appointed auditor of a company if he is an officer or servant of the company or of any other company which is a subsidiary company or a holding company of that company of any of the subsidiary companies of such a holding company; or if he is a partner of or in the employment of an officer or servant of the company or any such companies. Nor can a body corporate be appointed as an auditor of a company.

(b) (i) The principal duties of auditors consist of the common law duties of skill and care and those statutory duties contained in *CA 1948*. *S. 14 CA 1967* repeals and replaces with additional provisions *s. 162 CA 1948*. *S. 14(1)* of the Act requires that the auditors shall make a report to the members on the accounts examined by them, and on every balance sheet, every profit and loss account and all group accounts laid before the company in general meeting during their tenure of office. The general requirement is that the auditor's report must state whether the accounts of the company have been properly prepared in accordance with the Companies Acts and whether they give a true and fair view of the financial affairs of the company. *S. 14(4)* provides that the auditor is under a duty in preparing his report to carry out such investigations as will enable him to form an opinion in these respects; whether proper accounting records have been kept by the company and proper returns adequate for their audit received from branches not visited; and whether the balance sheet and profit and loss account are in agreement with the accounting records and returns. If the auditor is not satisfied in any such respect he must state this fact in his report. Likewise, if he fails to obtain all the necessary information and explanations which are required for the audit, he must qualify his report accordingly. A specific duty is laid on an auditor who resigns his appointment before the expiry of his term of office. *CA 1976* requires him to file a statement with his notice of resignation at the company's registered office (and the company must send a copy to the Registrar and every person entitled to notice of general meetings) to the effect that there are no circumstances connected with his resignation which ought to be made known to the company's members or creditors or, if there are such circumstances, an account of them. Additional detailed duties devolve upon auditors under *CA 1981*, including making reports in connection with the filing exemptions in respect of small and medium-sized companies, companies financing the purchase of or otherwise purchasing their own shares, and also a statutory duty to ensure that the directors' report is consistent with the financial statements and if not to state the fact in the audit report.

(ii) *CA 1976* gives the auditor greater rights to demand information and explanations from the company's officers to assist him in the discharge of the aforementioned statutory duties. *S. 14(5) CA 1967* gives the auditor right of access at all times to the books and accounts and vouchers of the company; additionally, he is empowered to require from the officers of the company such information and explanations as he thinks necessary for the purpose of his duties. That section confers no power on the auditor to require similar information in respect of a company's subsidiaries, but this omission is now rectified by *s. 18 CA 1976*. Further, as regards the collection of information from the officers of the company generally, *s. 19 CA 1976* creates a criminal offence of making a misleading, false or deceptive statement to an auditor when pursuing his statutory duties; this offence is additional to those under *s. 438 CA 1948* and *s. 5* of the *Perjury Act 1911*.

ANSWER D1

(i) A general meeting may only validly transact business of which adequate notice has been given. A special resolution is so defined as to require that its full text shall be set out in the notice convening the meeting: *s. 141(2) CA 1948*. But if the amendment would be within the scope of the notice and is 'not material' a special resolution may in principle perhaps be amended: *Torbock v Lord Westbury* (*1902*) (a decision of a period when procedure for passing special resolutions was different). Both A's amendments are changes of substance and not merely minor textual amendments: *Re Moorgate Mercantile Holdings* (*1980*) confirms that such an amendment cannot be avoided—it is such that the resolution will no longer be the one of which notice was given and if it is passed it will be void. All three members of the company were present and they could (under *s. 141(2)*) waive the 21 days' notice required and agree to deal with A's amended resolution as a new special resolution altogether. But apparently B and C were not prepared to agree to do this; they cannot be compelled to do so or deprived against their will of a 21 day period of notice of a new resolution.

(ii) If however B is held later to have erred in rejecting A's amendments the original resolution as passed is not valid either: *Henderson v Bank of Australasia* (*1890*). An alternative possible ground of invalidity is that a quorum was no longer present when the resolution was passed. This point depends on whether the articles of association follow *Article 53* of *Table A* which requires that a quorum, i.e. all three members personally present in this case, shall be present 'at the time when the meeting proceeds to business'. In such a case a resolution may be valid even if the quorum was no longer present when it was passed: *Re Hartley Baird Ltd* (*1954*). On the other hand the resolution would be invalid if either the articles required a quorum to be present throughout the meeting or if only one member was still present (he cannot constitute a meeting by himself: *Re London Flats Ltd* (*1969*)). A should be advised accordingly.

ANSWER D2

A company 'shall give its members notice' of a resolution of which special notice has been given to the company (*s. 142 CA 1948*), but it has been held that this is merely procedural, i.e. to ensure that if the resolution is to be considered at the meeting adequate notice shall be given to members: *Pedley v Inland Waterways Association Ltd* (*1977*).

Subject to special provision (if any) in the articles, a member, even if he is seeking to exercise statutory rights under *s. 184 CA 1948*, cannot compel the directors to include his resolution (of which special notice has been given) in the notice issued to members—unless of course the member can invoke *s. 140 CA 1948*, which provides that members who hold at least one twentieth of the voting rights (or at least one hundred members holding an average of at least £100 of paid up shares) can require the directors to include their resolution in the notice of AGM. In this case the member's requisition must be deposited with the company at least six weeks (special notice only requires four weeks) before the date of the meeting.

ANSWER D3

J has grounds for suspecting that the sale was at an undervalue and if so that the directors have been negligent. If the directors do not in their report, issued with the annual accounts, give a satisfactory explanation J could oppose the resolution for the adoption of the accounts, but the votes of Y Ltd will suffice to carry the resolution. J has no *locus standi* to sue the directors on behalf of the company for mere negligence: *Pavlides v Jensen* (*1956*). But he could do so if the directors (or Y Ltd which they represent) appear to have benefited, i.e. negligence *plus benefit* to the negligent controlling shareholder is equated with fraud: mere incompetence did not satisfy the test of 'oppression' for *s. 210 CA 1949; Re Five Minute Car Wash Service Ltd* (*1966*). *S. 210 CA 1948* has now been replaced by *s. 75 CA 1980* and the petitioner must now prove *unfairly prejudical conduct.* Whether mere incompetence amounts to *unfairly prejudicial conduct* is debatable but certainly the new provision is intended to include more cases than previously. He might as an alternative apply to the Department of Trade for an investigation on the grounds that (i) there has been misfeasance or (ii) members have not been given proper information—but the Department is not easily persuaded to exercise its powers in such a case. If, however, one of the directors has benefited, J could also allege (to the Department) that there is a fraudulent management: *s. 165* (*1*) (*b*) *CA 1948.*

S. 48 CA 1980 is designed to meet exactly this problem. It is concerned with substantial property transactions where either the directors or their *connected persons* are buyers of the company's property or sellers to the company. If the sale (or purchase) of the property is to (or by) a director or his connected person and concerns a substantial non-cash asset, the prior approval of the company in general meeting is required. A transaction will be for a substantial non-cash asset if its value exceeds £50,000 or 10% of the company's assets (subject to a minimum of £1,000). If a director is the sole beneficial owner of a company, the company will be a connected person (*s. 64 CA 1980*) for the purposes of *s. 48 CA 1980*. Failure to comply with *s. 48* leads to civil remedies and criminal sanctions but the remedies are given to the company. Thus, unless James can get the support of other shareholders, he will be unable to rescind the sale.

Moreover, if the directors of Y Ltd have been able to suppress opposition to a sale to a connected concern, this will strengthen James's claim that he should be permitted to bring a derivative action on the company's behalf. The case will then be more like *Daniels v Daniels* (*1978*) in which there was no evidence of fraud but one of the majority gained a personal benefit. The minority shareholder was allowed to sue to recoup for the company its loss.

ANSWER D4

(i) The company has no contractual obligation to repay the loan until the agreed 10-year period has expired. If nonetheless G has a justifiable grievance any claim he has is as a creditor and not as a shareholder. This fact would have disqualified G from obtaining relief under *s. 210 CA 1948*; *Re Bellador Silk Ltd* (*1965*). The new *s. 75 CA 1980* which replaces *s. 210 CA 1948* is for shareholders only and presumably this restricts its use to shareholders claiming in their capacity as shareholders and not as creditor or employees or otherwise. Alternatively, G could petition for a liquidation of the company on the just and equitable grounds: *s. 222(f) CA 1948*. In the liquidation he would prove as a creditor for the debt and would take priority over any repayment of capital to shareholders.

(ii) Excessive remuneration of directors at the expense of funds otherwise available to pay dividends was the example given by the Cohen Committee in 1945 when it recommended that *s. 210 CA 1948* be enacted. George could petition under *s. 75 CA 1980* on the basis of unfairly prejudicial conduct. Whether Henry's conduct would amount to this is a question of fact for the court to decide. If George were successful, the court has power to order what remedy it thinks fit, e.g. requiring Henry to purchase George's shares at a fair market value or to order Henry to pay a dividend if there are sufficient available profits.

Although George may succeed in an action for liquidation on the just and equitable ground (*s. 222(f) CA 1948*), his remedy would be liquidation and not payment of dividend. The court on liquidation would have no power to order Henry to repay some of the excessive remuneration to the company for the benefit of the ordinary shareholders, but the company would not be represented by the liquidator who might on behalf of the company sue Henry if there is any breach of director's duty by him.

ANSWER D5

The provisions of *Table A* (and of most public and many private companies' articles) on appointment and retirement of directors require that at each Annual General Meeting (i) any director appointed by the board since the last such meeting and (ii) one third of the other directors of the number nearest to one third (excluding any managing director) shall retire from office but may offer themselves for re-election: *Table A Articles 89 and 95*.

Under these rules all the three directors appointed since the last Annual General Meeting must retire and also the number nearest one third out of the four other directors (excluding the fifth who is managing director). One is the integral number nearest to one third of four.

Although the managing director is (*Table A Article 107*) excluded from retirement by rotation—and from the total number to be divided by three for this purpose—the chairman is subject to the same rules as other directors. It is immaterial that the four directors due to retire are full-time employees: the managing director alone is excluded as holder of an executive employment or office.

Unless otherwise agreed, out of the four directors subject to retirement under the rotation rules, the one who has held office longest since his last election or re-election will retire on this occasion: *Article 90*.

The question states that none of the directors had reached the age (of 70) at which he might have to retire under *s. 185 CA 1948*, although this section applies only in a public company.

ANSWER D6

Prior to *CA 1980*, unless the articles require that dividends shall be paid out of trading profits only (*Table A Article 116* however merely specifies 'profits' of any description), there was no legal objection to payment of dividend out of a realised capital profit: *Lubbock v British Bank of South America* (*1892*). It was not necessary to make good a loss on a fixed asset: *Verner v General & Commercial Investment Trust* (*1894*). But in calculating whether there was a capital profit available for dividend *all* fixed assets must be valued and any deficiency (of current value against book value) must be brought into the over-all calculation: *Foster v New Trinidad Lake Asphalt Co* (*1901*). *CA 1980* provides that a company may only make a distribution out of available profits defined as 'accumulated realised profits less accumulated realised losses: *s. 39 CA 1980*. This would mean that the company must make up the loss on Site A before paying out any dividend but could still use a realised capital profit for dividend payments. The surplus on Site B has not been realised by sale but is an *unrealised* surplus resulting from revaluation of a retained fixed asset. An unrealised surplus of this kind was possibly available for dividend: *Dimbula Valley* (*Ceylon*) *Tea Co Ltd v Laurie* (*1961*). But this view conflicts with a Scottish decision (*Westburn Sugar Refineries Ltd v IRC* (*1960*)) and has been overruled by statute *s. 39 CA 1980*. Accordingly there are two objections to the director's scheme, i.e. (i) the loss on Site A must be set off against the surplus on Site B, and (ii) the surplus on Site B is unrealised.

Moreover, there is no indication whether the company is private or public. If it were a public limited company, even though it had profits available for distribution, it could not do so if that would reduce its net assets below the aggregate of its called up share capital and undistributable reserves.

ANSWER D7

The most effective simplification of the group capital structure would be an exchange of new ordinary shares of the holding company for the minority shareholdings of the subsidiaries in suitable ratios. This could be effected under a scheme of arrangement which requires approval of the exchange by three-quarter majority (in value) at separate meetings of the holders of each class of share of each subsidiary followed by approval by the court: *ss. 206–208 CA 1948*. As an alternative procedure the holding company could simply offer its own shares in exchange for the minority shareholdings in subsidiaries. If the offer was accepted within four months by the holders of not less than 90% of the minority shareholdings of each subsidiary (taken separately), the holding company could then within the next following two months acquire compulsorily, but on the same terms as its original offer, the shares of non-accepting shareholders. The latter might however within one month of receiving a notice of intended acquisition apply to the court to set it aside: *s. 209(1) CA 1948* (but this is rarely done unless there is some manifest unfairness).

Tutorial note

An alternative method of simplification would be for the holding company to acquire the assets of the subsidiaries by a scheme under *s. 287 CA 1948*, but this method is rarely used because it can easily be upset by members or creditors who object. Similarly, individual internal simplification of the structure of each company by alteration of articles would be cumbersome and subject (in the case of variation of class rights) to the appeal to the court provided for by *s. 72 CA 1948*.

ANSWER D8

When the shares of non-accepting shareholders are acquired compulsorily under *s. 209(1) CA 1948*, the offeror must make the same terms available as were offered to the 90% or more of shareholders who accepted. Accordingly Growth must offer to non-acceptors (or arrange that Moneybank or some other third party does so) the alternative of an offer to buy for £5 in cash every five shares of Growth which the non-accepting shareholders of Dozy do not wish to retain: *Re Carlton Holdings (1971)*.

There is no rule of law which requires a take-over bidder to make this offer at least equal in value to the price paid in his purchase of other shares of the company in the market previously. But the Take-over Code does impose such a rule. In this case one Growth share (valued by the cash alternative of £5 for five Growth shares) is valued at £1 and so the bid (on a one for one share basis) is an offer for Dozy shares of £1 each in value. This infringes the Code since other shares have been purchased for £1.05: the Panel would require that the value of the offer should in some way be raised to a value of £1·05 for each Dozy share (e.g. one Growth share plus 5p in cash for each Dozy share).

The dissenting shareholders may apply to the court within one month from the date the offer was made for the court to refuse the bidder the right to acquire their shares compulsorily.

An individual is prohibited from dealing in quoted securities when he is in possession of inside information—i.e. unpublished price-sensitive information (*s. 68 CA 1980*), but a company is not so prohibited. It appears that Growth Plc may purchase shares on the market even though it is contemplating making a take-over bid, which could be regarded as inside information.

ANSWER D9

A company cannot reduce its share capital. This general principle is reflected in a number of rules relating to the raising and maintenance of capital, one of which is the rule that dividends can only be paid out of profits—i.e. profits available for distribution: *s. 39 CA 1980*. These are defined as 'accumulated realised profits less accumulated realised losses'. Thus the directors of Esk must bring forward the previous trading losses, and only if the profit of the fifth year is sufficient to wipe out the losses of the previous years can they declare a dividend, and then only of the excess.

Moreover, the directors of a company are obliged to consider the interests of the company—i.e. the shareholders and the employees. They should act in good faith in respect of both categories.

If Esk were a public limited company, there are two further provisions the directors must consider. (a) They can only pay a dividend out of profits available for distribution and only if net assets would not be reduced below the aggregate of the company's called-up share capital and its undistributable reserves: *s. 40 CA 1980*. The undistributable reserves are made up of the share premium account, the capital redemption reserve fund, unrealised profits and any other reserves retained by the company. It is unlikely in this case that the profit made by the company could make up the capital and provide sufficient available profits for a legal distribution. (b) As the company's net assets only represent half of the nominal value of the company's capital the directors should summon an extraordinary general meeting of the company to consider whether and if so what measures could be taken to deal with the situation. This is a new obligation imposed on directors of public limited companies by *CA 1980* as an additional capital maintenance provision: *s. 34 CA 1980*. It seems unlikely that the directors could make a dividend distribution whether Esk is a public or private company. If they did, they are in breach of their duties to the company, and any member who knows or has reasonable grounds for believing that the distribution is in breach shall be liable to repay the whole or part of the dividend paid in excess of these provisions: *s. 44 CA 1980*.

ANSWER D10

J could seek the support of other members holding sufficient shares (10% of the issued share capital is required) to requisition an EGM under *s. 132 CA 1948* and give special notice of his intention to propose resolutions for the removal from office of the directors and the appointment of more efficient and dynamic directors under *s. 184 CA 1948*. If however this course is or would be unsuccessful or is not what J requires, he could petition the court for a compulsory winding up on the just and equitable ground under *s. 222(f) CA 1948*. His prospects of success however are poor since the recognised grounds do not exist, i.e. the substratum had gone, his disapproval of the directors' performance is not a state of 'deadlock' and there is no apparent evidence of unfairly prejudicial conduct. Non-payment of dividends alone cannot be complained of as it is a business decision delegated to the board: *Re Jermyn Street Turkish Baths Ltd* (*1971*).

It would need to be coupled with other 'prejudicial' conduct before justifying either a *s. 75* order or a winding up.

John is of course not confined to grounds accepted in the past: *Ebrahimi v Westbourne Galleries Ltd* (*1973*), but a commercial dispute over management and profitability is not the sort of situation in which a remedy is normally available under *s. 222(f)* (or under *s. 75 CA 1980*). On technical points however J is in a sound position, i.e. he inherited his shares from a previous holder now dead, and so the six month rule does not apply: *s. 224(1)(a)(ii) CA 1948*. The company is apparently solvent and so J has an 'interest' in obtaining his proportion of the available surplus to be distributed when the company's debts (in a liquidation) have been paid.

ANSWER D11

(a) A committee of inspection is a committee of representatives of creditors and contributories, usually in equal number, appointed in a compulsory or a creditors' voluntary winding up. The purpose of the committee is to assist and supervise the liquidator and act as a liaison body between the liquidator and the members and creditors.

In a compulsory winding up the committee is appointed by the court on the recommendation of the first meetings of creditors and contributories called by the Official Receiver: *s. 252 CA 1948*. In a creditors' voluntary winding up the meetings of members and of creditors called at the commencement of the winding up may each appoint up to five persons to the committee of inspection: *s. 295 CA*

1948. Any replacements of original members are appointed in the same way. Members of the committee are fiduciaries and not entitled to payment except for out of pocket expenses; nor may they purchase company assets without the leave of the court.

(b) A committee of inspection meets once a month (unless the members agree otherwise). Any member may call a meeting when he thinks it necessary: *ss. 253 and 295 CA 1948*.

ANSWER D12

It is the duty of the liquidator to realise the assets of the company. He will no doubt consider selling the lease. Meanwhile the company's liability to pay rent under the lease continues though it is evident that no money is available to pay it. If the lease of the factory is unsaleable the liquidator is likely to apply to the court for leave to disclaim the lease: *s. 323 CA 1948*. The lease is then surrendered and the factory reverts to the landlord's control. He would become a creditor of the company for future loss of revenue as well as for accrued rent. The liquidator may apply for leave to disclaim at any time within 12 months from the commencement of the winding up. But Property may serve a notice on the liquidator requiring him to state within four weeks whether he intends to apply for disclaimer. Unless he replies that he will do so, he loses the right to disclaim. In practice the liquidator and the landlord would attempt to reach agreed terms for surrender of the lease without resort to *s. 323*, which is a procedure of final resort.

ANSWER D13

S. 184 CA 1948 provides that a director may always be removed by ordinary resolution of the company. The facts of the problem make it clear that the company has previously traded in the form of a partnership. This brings it within the principle in *Ebrahimi v Westbourne Galleries Ltd* (*1973*) where the House of Lords held that a company may be dissolved on the just and equitable ground (*s. 222(f) CA 1948*) where, had the business been a partnership, it would have been dissolved under the *Partnership Act 1890*.

In *Ebrahimi*, E, who brought the petition, had with Mr Nazar originally operated the business of selling Persian carpets as a partnership but had later incorporated the business. They were the first directors and later Nazar's son, George, was also appointed a director. Nazar and his son started to quarrel with Ebrahimi and purported to remove him.

The House of Lords held unanimously that Ebrahimi was entitled to a winding up order. The Law Lords, whilst recognising the right to remove a director, held that a petition to wind up on the just and equitable ground would succeed if the petitioning director could show that the business was operated on the understanding that he would be entitled to participate in the management. This principle would apply here.

Another possibility that should be considered is *s. 75 CA 1980*, which provides a remedy to a member where the company's affairs have been conducted in an unfairly prejudicial manner.

However, this section would probably not help Michael as he has not been prejudiced *qua* member but rather *qua* director. This was the situation under *s. 210 CA 1948* which *s. 75* replaces. The remedy is intended to be for aggrieved *members*.

ANSWER D14

Apart from the appointment of an inspector (or as is usual joint inspectors) to investigate the affairs of the company under *s. 165 CA 1948*, the Department of Trade may give directions to a company requiring it to produce books and documents: *s. 109 CA 1967*. This is the normal first step so that the Department may have sufficient information upon which to reach a decision whether to appoint inspectors under *s. 165*.

If the Department decides to take further action it may appoint inspectors on various grounds, such as suspected fraud, illegality or oppression or merely because (as appears to be the case here) the members of the company have not been given the information with respect to its affairs which they might reasonably expect: *s. 165(b)(iii)*. This was the ground for the investigation of Pergamon Press Ltd in circumstances very like those described in the question. The company cannot compel the Department to disclose the evidence which leads it to take these steps: *Re Norwest Holst Ltd (1978)*.

It is the duty of any officer or agent of the company and any other person who is in possession of any information concerning the company's affairs to produce for the inspectors any books or documents in their custody and to attend before the inspectors if required to do so: *s. 167 CA 1948* as amended by *s. 87 CA 1981*.

If any officer or agent of the company refuses to produce to the inspectors any book or document or refuses to attend before the inspectors when required to do so or refuses to answer questions put by the inspectors, the inspectors may refer the matter to the court who will enquire into the case and may punish the officer or agent as if he had been guilty of contempt of court.

A full scale investigation of affairs can be very damaging to a company and might then reveal nothing; an investigation of books and papers will reveal confidentially whether anything is amiss to justify a full enquiry and is therefore often preferable as a first step.

ANSWER D15

If a special resolution is passed the Department of Trade is *obliged* to conduct an investigation. This does not appear to be the case here. The Department of Trade may conduct an investigation at the suit of 200 shareholders or shareholders who hold one tenth of the issued shares or where the Department itself considers that the affairs of the company have been carried on fraudulently and unlawfully or in a way unfairly prejudicial to some of the members or where it considers that the members have not been given all the information they might reasonably expect: *s. 164 CA 1948*.

Thus if the complaining shareholders are 200 in number or one tenth in proportion or if the Department itself considers an investigation should be carried out, this may happen. It should be noted that an investigation is not compulsory.

Many famous companies have had their affairs investigated, e.g. Savoy Hotel, Rolls Royce, Pergamon Press.

Where an investigation is set up it is usual for the Secretary of State to appoint two inspectors. One of these is generally a senior accountant, the other a senior lawyer.

The proceedings of the inspectors are *inquisitorial*, that is to say the inspectors do not actually decide anything. They act merely as sleuths.

The affairs which the inspectors investigate include all matters relating to the management, assets, profits or losses of the company and extend to the affairs of any related company.

The inspectors can require all officers and agents (and this includes the auditors!) past and present of any company being investigated to attend the investigation and to answer questions and to produce any documents in their custody or control.

The investigation is conducted in private and the inspectors are masters in their own house and virtually free to fix their own rules of procedure.

When the investigation is over the inspectors' report is sent to the Department of Trade and their report is generally published. The report itself is '*admissible in any legal proceedings as evidence of the opinion of the inspectors in relation to any matter contained in the report*': *s. 171 CA 1948*. This has given rise to much criticism as no formal charges are made and there is no privilege against self incrimination. Furthermore, the individual has no opportunity of challenging the evidence given by others.

However, Department of Trade investigators may, through their very existence, deter the unscrupulous. Moreover, the Department's report may ferret out information which a single shareholder would have found quite impossible to discover. This is most important for it is information about the affairs of the company which is the raw material which the shareholders will need to mould any case against the company's officers.

The Department may as a consequence of the report either petition for the winding up of the company or bring proceedings in the name of the company against its officers. The Department of Trade may thus relieve the shareholders of the financial burden of bringing legal proceedings.

ANSWER D16

The rules of bankruptcy apply to priority in payment of debts of an insolvent company in liquidation (*s. 317 CA 1948*). *Insolvency Act 1976 Sch. 1*) raises certain financial limits imposed by *CA 1948*.

(a) The bank's security is equal to the amount of its debt (presumably including expenses of sale). As legal mortgagee the bank could sell; alternatively the liquidator might redeem the premises on payment of £30,000. However the matter is settled, the bank as secured creditor obtains £30,000 from the available assets.

(b) (i) Smith's floating charge might possibly be set aside under *s. 322 CA 1948* if it was created within the twelve months before the liquidation began and the company was not solvent at that time. But the question implies that Smith's loan of £15,000 was made at the time of (or after) the charge was created and in consideration of it. If so, the charge (since it was duly registered) is valid. On that basis Smith is at risk only to the extent that preferential debts cannot be paid in full out of uncharged assets. As the remaining assets exceed Smith's secured loan by £5,000 and the preferential debts cannot exceed £3,800 (see (c) below), it would appear that Smith will be paid his £15,000 loan in full out of his security.

(ii) If Smith earned his salary as management remuneration and not as director's fees, his claim is a preferential debt within the limits referred to in (c) below (*Re Beeton & Co* (*1913*)).

(iii) The director's fees of £1,000 are an ordinary unsecured debt ranking with those of the trade creditors in (d) below.

(c) The wages of any *clerk or servant* are preferential debts subject to a limit of four months' arrears and £800 in each case: *s. 319*(*2*) *CA 1948* (as amended). The employees' wages and Smith's salary would be preferential within those limits.

(d) An unpaid dividend is a deferred debt and is paid only if all ordinary debts have been paid in full. Clearly nothing will be available for the dividends of £2,000.

(e) The unsecured trade creditors and Smith in respect of his director's fees of £1,000 and employees (including Smith) in respect of that part of their salary or wages which is not preferential will share rateably whatever is left after the preferential debts have been paid.

ANSWER D17

(a) Special notice (*s. 142 CA 1948*) is required on the following occasions:

(i) to remove a director from office under *s. 184 CA 1948* or to appoint someone in his place;

(ii) under *s. 15 CA 1976* special notice must be given of a resolution to (a) appoint as auditor a person other than the retiring auditor, (b) to fill a casual vacancy in the office of auditor, (c) to reappoint as auditor a retiring auditor who was appointed by the directors to fill a casual vacancy, or (d) to remove an auditor from office before the expiry of his term. In effect whenever there is a change of auditors special notice must be given of intention to appoint the new auditor at the first general meeting concerned with his appointment;

(iii) to appoint or reappoint a director who has attained the age of 70: *s. 185 CA 1948*. This rule applies only to public companies and to private companies which are subsidiaries of public companies provided in either case that the rule may be excluded by the articles of association.

The special notice is a 28 day notice to the company of intention to move the resolution at the impending general meeting. In cases falling under *ss. 184 and 15* the director or auditor has a statutory right to be heard in his own defence both by written representations circulated to members and at the meeting itself.

(b) (i) In any of the cases mentioned in (a) above, the resolution will be validly passed if the required 28 days notice has been given to the company and the statutory protection provided by *s. 184* or *s. 15* to enable the director or auditor to justify himself has been observed.

On receiving special notice the company is required to give notice of the resolution to members in convening the meeting, or if that is not possible by newspaper advertisement. In either case 21 days' notice should be given to members: *s. 142 CA 1948*.

The resolution is carried by a simple majority of votes cast.

(ii) A special resolution is one which is passed by a three quarters majority of the votes cast at a general meeting convened by a 21 days' notice specifying the intention to pass the resolution as a special resolution. There is provision for waiver of 21 days' notice with the consent of 95% (in votes) of those entitled to attend and vote: *s. 141 CA 1948*.

ANSWER D18

If C is correct in thinking that the company is selling a valuable asset for less than its real value the immediate loss will fall on the company. Under the rule in *Foss v Harbottle* (*1843*) it is for the company, not its individual shareholders, to take action to prevent the loss occurring or to recover damages from those who have caused the loss. Since C owns one third of the share capital he has more than the one tenth required by *s. 132 CA 1948* for requisition an Extraordinary General Meeting. His only available course of action is to requisition a meeting, if A and B as directors will not heed his protests.

For two reasons C will get little satisfaction by causing a meeting to be held. First, A and B are not defrauding the company and may according to *North-West Transportation Co Ltd v Beatty* (*1887*) use their votes to approve their own action. Secondly, if the articles of association follow the model of *Table A Article 80*, the company's business is entrusted to the directors and a general meeting (even if C could command a majority of votes) cannot instruct the directors as to how they should use their powers: *Salmon v Quin and Axtens Ltd* (*1909*) (though it could remove them from office under *s. 184*).

C could petition on the basis of *s. 75 CA 1980*, which replaces the infamous *s. 210 CA 1948*. *S. 75* permits a shareholder to petition the court for a remedy where the affairs of the company are conducted in an *unfairly prejudicial manner*. A shareholder may complain under this section even if the action has not yet been taken but is only proposed. Moreover, the requirement of *s. 75*, unfairly prejudicial, is thought to be easier to show than oppression, and finally, the new section is not tied up with a winding up on the just and equitable ground. It is likely that a petition under *s. 75* would succeed.

The facts of the question are somewhat similar to those of *Pavlides v Jensen* (*1956*) where a shareholder complained of negligence of the directors in selling an asset for less than its value (in his opinion); the rule in *Foss v Harbottle* was applied.

If however A and B had a substantial interest in the firm to which the painting is to be sold, they would be using their control of Fine Arts Ltd to defraud the company of part of its assets (if C is right in thinking that the picture is worth £100,000 and not £50,000). This is one of the exceptions to *Foss v Harbottle* and a single shareholder may in these circumstances sue in a derivative action on behalf of the company (*Cook v Deeks* (*1916*)) to safeguard its interest. If the directors use their powers to enrich themselves actual fraud need not be proved: *Daniels v Daniels* (*1978*). C, if successful, can recover his legal costs from the company: *Wallersteiner v Moir* (*1975*).

A company cannot enter into an arrangement with its directors or their connected persons for acquisition by them of a *substantial non-cash asset* from the company unless approved by a resolution of the company in general meeting: *s. 48 CA 1980*. A substantial non-cash asset is one which exceeds £50,000 or 10% of the company's relevant assets but is not less than £1,000. This painting may be a substantial non-cash asset and if A and B were partners in a firm, approval of the transaction would be necessary.

Failure to obtain the necessary approval renders the arrangement voidable by the company and the persons in default liable in damages for any loss suffered by the company.

ANSWER D19

(a) A petition for winding up a company by order of the court may be presented by a creditor if the company is unable to pay its debts: *s. 222(e) CA 1948*. A company is deemed to be unable to pay its debts if:
(i) a creditor to whom the company is liable on a debt of at least £200 (*Sch. 1 Insolvency Act 1976*) has left a written demand for payment at the registered office and the company has not, within the ensuing three weeks, paid the debt or offered satisfactory security;
(ii) a creditor in whose favour judgement has been given, has obtained an order for execution, i.e. enforcement of the judgement by payment from the company's assets and this can not be effected;
(iii) the court taking account of the company's contingent and prospective liabilities is satisfied that it is unable to pay its debts: *s. 223 CA 1948*.

(b) The 'just and equitable' ground for compulsory winding up is the last and most general of the grounds specified by *s. 222 CA 1948*. To fall under this head a just and equitable ground need not be of the same kind (*ejusdem generis*) with the other five and may also be a novel ground such as has not been relied on in any previous case: *Ebrahimi v Westbourne Galleries Ltd* (*1973*).

One example of the just and equitable ground is where the company has been formed for one specific purpose only, e.g., to exploit a patented process for making coffee from dates, and is unable to carry out that purpose as defined in its objects clause: *Re German Date Coffee Co* (*1882*). It is then said that its only main object or *substratum* has failed. If there is more than one object the rule does not apply unless all those objects have failed.

A second example is a small company in which relations between the directors have deteriorated to the point at which they are unable to work together in managing the company (*Ebrahimi's Case* above) or even to communicate directly with each other: *Re Yenidje Tobacco Co Ltd* (*1916*). In such cases the court is lifting the veil of incorporation by looking through the company to the directors who manage it to decide whether deadlock between them, as in the *Yenidje Case*, or unfair use of legal powers (in *Ebrahimi's Case* power to remove a director from office under *s. 184*) make it just and equitable to put the company into liquidation.

ANSWER D20

Under *ss. 222*(*e*) *and 223*(*a*) *CA 1948* (as amended by the *Insolvency Act 1976*) a creditor may present a petition for the compulsory winding up of a company on the basis of an outstanding debt claimed by him of not less than £200. He must first present to the company at its registered office a written and signed demand for payment. If the company during the next three weeks fails either to pay the debt or to offer security to the reasonable satisfaction of the creditor he may present his petition.

It is however open to the company to oppose the petition. If the company can satisfy the court that it has a defence to the creditor's claim for debt which is likely to succeed the court will decline to reach a decision on the creditor's claim for debt but will dismiss the petition and leave the creditor to seek a judgement for debt which, when obtained, is a final decision on the matter in dispute (except where the company later contends that the judgement debt was incurred in an *ultra vires* transaction).

The court will also consider the objections to the petition of other creditors. If the company owes more to the objectors than to the petitioning creditor the court is likely to dismiss the petition. But in this as in all other matters the court will consider the merits of opposing parties' cases and has a discretion to make or refuse an order.

(a) A counterclaim by the company if it appears to have some substance would probably lead the court to dismiss the petition. That was the outcome in *Re London and Paris Banking Corporation* (*1874*) where the company admitted that part of the amount claimed was due and tendered payment but denied liability on the balance.

(b) Although the opposing creditor is apparently owed a larger sum (£5,000) he is, as director of the company, not concerned simply with the payment of his debt. He may be more concerned to keep the company in being as a going concern. In *Mann v Goldstein* (*1968*), where the petitioners were directors and shareholders and their claims were in dispute, the court treated them as not established creditors. By analogy, objections from such a source would probably not be regarded as coming from a creditor in the ordinary sense. It was held in *Re Southard & Co* (*1979*) that the court need not follow the wishes of the largest creditor but may consider the reasons for the petition and objections—the courts have consistently taken more cognisance of the wishes of outside creditors than those of directors or shareholders in the company itself.

ANSWER D21

(a) The charge in favour of the director appears to be valid since it was registered under *s. 95 CA 1948*. As the charge was created more than 12 months before the commencement of the winding up, it cannot be challenged under *s. 322* (and in any case it appears to satisfy the requirements of validity under that section).

As it is a floating charge, the liquidator may have recourse to the assets charged to pay preferential debts (if any) if there are no uncharged assets available for its payment. Subject to that the creditor is entitled to repayment of his loan out of his security and any balance left over is available for the unsecured creditors. In the circumstances it is immaterial that the creditor is also a director. Even if the articles do not sanction contracts between directors and the company, the right of the company is merely to rescind the loan contract, i.e. to repay the money—which leads to a similar result by a different route.

(b) The repayment of the overdraft which enabled a director to recover property pledged in support of his guarantee could probably be set aside as a fraudulent preference under *s. 320 CA 1948*. It occurred within six months of the commencement of the winding up; it was apparently a voluntary act; and it had the purpose and effect of preferring one creditor over others. The facts are somewhat similar to those of *Re Kushler* (*1943*). If the bank was ordered to repay the money to the company it would certainly have a personal claim against the managing director under his guarantee for any part of the overdraft not repaid in the course of liquidation, but could not recover the title deeds: *s. 321 CA 1948*.

(c) The payment to a creditor who threatened legal proceedings is not a voluntary act of preferring that creditor to others. For that reason the payment could not set aside under *s. 320: Sharp v Jackson* (*1899*).

ANSWER D22

The simplest and most obvious procedure is for X Ltd to make a written offer to the preference shareholders of Y Ltd offering ordinary shares of X in exchange for their preference shares of Y. If acceptances are received within a period of four months from the holders of at least 90% of the preferences shares of Y, X could then under *s. 209 CA 1948* serve notice during the ensuing two months on the non-accepting shareholders of the intention of X to acquire their shares compulsorily on the terms of the offer. The non-accepting shareholders could however within one month of receiving this notice apply to the court to set aside the proposed acquisition.

The main risk here is that X Ltd will be unable to secure acceptances from the required 90%. In normal circumstances the court would not uphold the objections of a minority of 10% or less if 90% had accepted.

The offer for the preference shares is treated as an offer for a separate class. It is probably immaterial that the offer is made by a company which already holds the ordinary shares of Y. But the court would be free, as in *Re Bugle Press Ltd* (*1960*), to lift the veil of incorporation and consider whether company structure was being used in some unfair fashion. But it does not appear to be so in this case.

The effect of the exchange would be that holders of preference shares of Y Ltd would in the end hold ordinary shares of X Ltd instead. This could also be effected by a scheme of arrangement under *s. 206* by which the preference shares would be cancelled and ordinary shares of X issued to replace them. For this procedure X Ltd and Y Ltd would submit a scheme of arrangement, setting out the details, and an explanatory circular (*s. 207*) to the court for approval and ask for an order to convene a meeting of the preference shareholders of Y Ltd to approve the scheme. If a resolution approving the scheme were carried by a three quarters majority the court could (*s. 208*) make an order to approve and give effect to the scheme. But any dissenting minority would have the opportunity of submitting its objections to the court before the court took its final decision. Again the court would be unlikely to disapprove a scheme which had been approved by a three quarters majority. It might however require X to purchase the shares in Y held by the objectors for cash instead of acquiring them under the scheme by share exchange.

The advantage of a scheme of arrangement under *s. 206* over acquisition under *s. 209* is that the former only requires approval by three quarters of the votes cast by those who choose to vote whereas *s. 209* requires 90% acceptance from all preference shareholders. Apart from the active opposition there may be some who are indifferent and would neither vote (abstainers do not have to be counted) nor accept (but non-acceptance is in effect a refusal). A second minor advantage of *s. 206* is a saving in stamp duty, i.e. the preference shares are cancelled by court order instead of being transferred.

The disadvantage of *s. 206* in this case is that the procedure is slow and the documentation of legal action are expensive. Under *s. 206* there must be two applications to the court at different stages; under *s. 209* there need be none and if application is made to the court the costs fall on the objectors (unless they succeed and are awarded their costs).

ANSWER D23

Although a company is not made bankrupt it is subject to bankruptcy rules governing priority of debts if the company is wound up on grounds of insolvency: *s. 317 CA 1948*. Leaving aside the special cases of secured debts and judgement debts, bankruptcy rules classify debts in order of priority as preferential, ordinary and deferred. Each category must be paid in full before assets are applied in discharge of debts in a lower order of priority.

Debts are classified as preferential by statute. The more important preferential debts of a company are:

(a) one year's corporation tax for a financial year selected by the Inland Revenue from the period on or before 5th April preceding the commencement of winding up;
(b) VAT, rates, National Insurance contributions and employees' income tax deducted under PAYE rules for the most recent year;
(c) wages and salaries of employees subject to a maximum of four months' arrears and £800 in any one case and also accrued holiday pay (the limit was raised from £200 to £800 by the *Insolvency Act 1976*).

There are three types of circumstances in which it is relevant to determine whether a debt is preferential. First, it is the duty of the liquidator to pay preferential debts before he pays any others. Hence he must obviously be able to identify them as preferential. Secondly, a person who assists a company to pay a preferential debt may himself then rank as a preferential creditor. This is the position of a surety for a preferential debt who pays it for the company. A person who lends money to pay wages and salaries is, to the extent that they are preferential debts as defined in (c) above, a preferential creditor for his loan. Thirdly, if other assets are insufficient to discharge preferential debts in full, the liquidator may use property subject to a floating charge for this purpose, i.e. the secured creditor cannot enforce his floating charge until preferential debts have been paid, if necessary out of the property over which his charge is given.

ANSWER D24

The effect of winding up varies according to the type of winding up. In particular a compulsory winding up order is retrospective to the date on which the petition for winding up was first presented to the court (and this date is the commencement date of the winding up). If however the company had already gone into voluntary liquidation first, the order for compulsory winding up is retrospective back to the date on which the voluntary winding up began: *s. 229 CA 1948*. A voluntary winding up commences from the passing of either an ordinary, or a special, or an extraordinary resolution. Voluntary winding up is either a members' or a creditors' winding up.

(i) The powers of the directors cease in a compulsory winding up but not with retrospective effect to the date of commencement. In a voluntary winding up the powers of the directors cease unless they are invited to continue in office: *ss. 285/296 CA 1948.*

(ii) In a compulsory winding up the staff are automatically dismissed but may be re-employed by the liquidator. A voluntary winding up does not always have that effect.

(iii) The title to the company's remaining assets remains with the company and does not pass to the liquidator although he has control of them. In a compulsory winding up any disposition of the company's property made after the date of commencement (which is retrospective) is void unless the court approves: *s. 227 CA 1948.*

(iv) No transfer of shares can be made except with special approval in any types of winding up. This again is retrospective in a compulsory winding up: *ss. 227/282 CA 1948.*

(v) Any floating charge crystallises on winding up. It may however be invalid under *s. 322* or as a fraudulent preference under *s. 320* if created within twelve or as the case may be six months of commencement.

(vi) In a compulsory winding up any legal action by or against the company is automatically halted unless the court approves its continuation. In a voluntary winding up the liquidator may apply to the court for an order to stay any action pending against the company: *s. 307 CA 1948.*

ANSWER D25

The directors of Pork Pies Ltd are in breach of their duty not to put themselves in a position of conflict of interest and duty. As directors they should obtain the highest price possible for the sale of the business (their duty to the company) but obviously they hope to get the business at the lowest possible price for Rashers Ltd (in their own interest). Whether or not there is actual conflict of interest and duty is irrelevant; the possibility of a conflict is sufficient to constitute a breach. The directors are, therefore, in breach of this duty.

Directors, however, only owe their duties to the company and not to the individual members. Thus, the company is the only proper plaintiff in an action against the directors for breach of their duty. The directors are the agents of the company for the purpose of taking legal action—it is highly unlikely that they will take proceedings against themselves.

Squealer could requisition a general meeting (he would require a 10% shareholding to insist on a meeting) to propose the removal of the directors (an ordinary resolution—50% of the votes would be required and he must comply with the rules regarding special notice). He could then secure the removal of the old directors and the appointment of more pliant directors who could take proceeding against the old directors to recover the loss suffered by the company: *Regal (Hastings) Ltd v Gulliver (1942).* If the directors also held shares in Pork Pies Ltd they could use these votes to prevent their own removal. Moreover, certain breaches of fiduciary duty are ratifiable by ordinary resolution and the directors might try to ratify this breach again using their own shares, if any.

Where a breach involves an appropriation of company property (or a minority shareholder's property), it is not capable of ratification. In this case the breach consists of a sale at an undervalue to another company and this would probably consitute an appropriation of corporate property.

If Squealer could not get the support of the majority of shareholders to a removal of the directors he could attempt to bring an action on behalf of the company against the directors. This would be a minority derivative action. Squealer would have to show fraud, i.e. appropriation of corporate property (discussed above), and that the wrongdoers were in control.

If Squealer were successful, any remedy (and therefore the proceeds of the action) would belong to the company not to Squealer, thus recognising that it was in fact the company's own action, i.e. derived from the company.

The other alternatives available to Squealer are to be found in statute. Squealer could petition the court under *s. 75 CA 1980* on the grounds that the affairs of the company were being conducted in an unfairly prejudicial manner. Under the old *s. 210 CA 1948* petition for oppression, mere negligence in valuing property was insufficient for oppression, but in this case there is more than negligence (the directors are to benefit themselves) and the petitioner only needs to show unfairly prejudicial conduct, not oppression, and this is presumably easier to prove.

Squealer could petition for the liquidation of the company on the just and equitable ground, *s. 222(f) CA 1948*, i.e. if the court considers it just and equitable to wind the company up. Such an action might be of no great help as Squealer's shareholding will be reduced in value because of the breach by the directors. Under *s. 75* on the other hand, the court has very wide powers and may make any order it thinks fit.

As the sale of the business to Rashers Ltd is a contract in which the directors are interested, i.e. as directors and shareholders in Rashers, they are required to disclose the nature of their interest to the board under *s. 199 CA 1948*. They need not say to what extent they are interested, merely that they have an interest. Failure to comply with this provision gives Squealer no right to bring proceedings but the directors may be fined (*CA 1980* removed the upper limit of £100).

The transaction might also be a substantial property transaction within *s. 48 CA 1980* and voidable at the option of the company if the shareholders consent is not obtained. Again, this provides Squealer with no direct remedy.

ANSWER D26

(a) *Dancing studio transactions*

Loan: S. 49 CA 1980 generally prohibits loans and similar transactions by all companies to directors and also to persons connected to them, subject to limited exceptions. Although the loan was not granted to Mrs Botchit herself, who is a director, Byron may fall into the category of a person connected with her. He is stated to be her dancing partner, and on the information given, they could also be partners in the dance studio. The business partner of a director is a 'connected person' according to *s. 64(1)(a) CA 1980.*

All loans to directors' connected persons are not automatically forbidden, but the above loan does not fall within any of the exemptions provided by *s. 50.*

Three consequences flow from this loan. In *ss. 52 and 53*, both civil and criminal penalties apply to both Mrs Botchit and Byron. The loan is voidable at the instance of the company and in addition both parties are jointly and severally liable to pay over any gain and reimburse any loss incurred to the company. There are also criminal penalties of fines and/or imprisonment for Mrs Botchit, and for Byron if he encouraged her to grant the loan, knowing and believing it was prohibited. There are certain limited defences available.

The third consequence is that, according to *s. 54*, the loan must be disclosed in the company's accounts, even if the loan is in contravention of the Act. As Mrs Botchit has taken care not to reveal the loan, no note will have appeared in the accounts presumably prepared prior to UGB's take-over, thus contravening the disclosure provisions. This is in itself a breach of *CA 1948* requirements on directors to ensure accurate financial statements.

Contract: The contract to supply beers may be one which also requires disclosure. If Mrs Botchit has a financial stake in the studio, she may, therefore, have a material interest in the contract. *S. 60* widens *s. 199 CA 1948* which covers disclosure to the Board by a director of interests in contracts to which the company is a party. Although this generally applies to contracts entered after the appointed day, transitional provisions may catch this particular contract if made in the financial year prior to the appointed day.

According to *s. 63*, Mrs Botchit should give notice of her interest to her fellow directors, and it is up to them to decide if the interest is sufficiently material to require disclosure in the company's accounts. Non-disclosure would again be a breach of *CA 1948* duty to ensure accurate financial statements.

(b) *Credit arrangements with Brian*

Car: Firstly, the arrangement relating to the Maserati could well be caught in the restrictions on substantial property transactions in *s. 48 1980.* Although Brian has not received the car as an outright gift, the disposal of a non-cash asset owned by the company includes the creation of an interest in the asset: *s. 87(1)(4)(6).*

There are three possible escape routes for Brian. A transaction is exempt if made before the appointed day. However, the arrangement is presumably meant to continue in being after the appointed day, and, of course, any renewal or substitute arrangements would be caught. There is also an exception based on value. According to *s. 48(1)* and *(2)*, if the value is greater than £1,000 but less than the lower of £50,000 or 10% of the amount of the company's relevant assets, the arrangement will be exempt. This can only be ascertained by applying rules in *s. 87(1)* to calculate the relevant assets. Finally, a resolution of the company in GM prior to the arrangement and in approval of it will always prevail.

Assuming the arrangement is in contravention of *s. 48*, it will be voidable at the instance of the company: *s. 48(3)*. Furthermore, both Bert and Brian will be liable to account to the company for any gain or indemnify it for loss (*s. 48(4)*), and there is no defence available to them.

Even if *s. 48* does not apply to the arrangement, it could still be caught by *s. 49* restrictions on credit transactions entered into by relevant companies. No such company can enter into a credit transaction as creditor for a director, which covers *inter alia* HP agreements and the hiring of goods in return for periodical payments: *s. 65(2)*.

Considering the probable value of the arrangement, full details should appear in a company's financial statements, especially as the arrangement is likely to be in contravention of either *s. 48* or *s. 49*. The sanction for non-disclosure is again as appears in (a), and the more important civil and criminal penalties for breach of *s. 48* and *s. 49* also apply.

Credit card: Brian's use of the company card again brings him within the ambit of *s. 49* on restricted credit arrangements. This time the prohibited arrangement is a *quasi-loan*, as defined by *s. 65(2)(a)*, i.e. the payment or reimbursement of expenditure by a creditor company on behalf of a debtor on terms that the latter or a third party is liable to reimburse the creditor. This, therefore, covers a director buying goods on a company's credit card. The general civil and criminal penalties under *s. 49* would thus apply.

Brian's only hope is that he can make use of an exception given by *s. 50*. Any company is permitted to provide a director with funds to meet business expenditure. This may, therefore, cover the purchase of business suits and the reception provisions, and the limit for permissible expenditure is as high as £10,000. However, in order to take advantage of this, the arrangement must have the prior approval of the company in GM or at least retrospective approval by the next AGM. If these conditions are not met, the loan must be repaid within six months of the relevant meeting. Therefore, Brian's reluctant offer to repay the debt next year may prove insufficient.

CA 1948 requires directors to take reasonable steps to ensure that financial statements contain accurate particulars of certain loans and interest in contracts. In order to remedy the deficiencies in the disclosure provisions, *CA 1980* contains eleborate rules in *ss. 54 and 60* to disclosure in the accounts of both public and private companies of information about transactions regulated by *ss. 48 and 49*, and about any other dealings in which a director has a material interest. The general duty still rests on directors, but in default the auditors are required by *s. 59* to insert in their report full particulars of all relevant matters are far as they are reasonably able to do so.

Details must be disclosed in relation to the Botchit family's arrangements. As disclosure appears to have been ignored or avoided, it would probably be up to the auditor to reveal in his report full details of the loan to Byron; any interest of Mrs Botchit in the beer contract if material is aggregated with the above loan; and Brian's Maserati, credit card and any other arrangements for himself and connected persons.

ANSWER D27

The statutory powers of disclaimer of a liquidator are contained in *s. 323 CA 1948*.

(a) The power is exercisable only by a company liquidator and he must first obtain leave of the court to exercise it in any particular case.

The liquidator may disclaim within twelve months of the commencement of the winding up or any longer period allowed by the court. If however he first became aware of the property to be disclaimed more than one month after the winding up began, the twelve months runs from the date on which he first became aware of it. Any person interested in property which could be disclaimed may serve on the liquidator a notice requiring him to decide whether he will apply for leave to disclaim; the liquidator must then state within 28 days of the notice (subject to any extension by the court) whether he will apply (or in the case of a burdensome contract disclaim it within that period); if the liquidator does not do so he loses his right to disclaim altogether.

(b) The property which may be disclaimed is land subject to onerous convenants, shares or stocks of companies, unprofitable contracts and any other property which is not readily saleable because it is subject to burdens or liabilities.

(c) The purpose of the right of disclaimer is to enable the liquidator to rid the company of property which is likely to cost the company more than it will bring in.

(d) Any person who suffers by the disclaimer may claim for his loss in the liquidation as a creditor (i.e. he will get a dividend if funds permit) or in certain circumstances have the property vested in him. In practice the liquidator is expected to settle these matters by negotiation so that formal disclaimer is usually unnecessary.

ANSWER D28

The main provisions of *CA 1948* on records of meeting are contained in *ss. 145 and 146*.

(a) Every company must keep minutes of the proceedings of its general meetings, and of meetings of its directors and managers. The minutes are to be entered in minute books kept for that purpose. If the minute books are in loose-leaf form adequate precautions must be taken against falsification: *s. 436*. The minutes are thus intended to be a permanent record.

(b) The minutes when signed by the chairman of the meeting or of the next succeeding meeting are evidence of the proceedings. Unless the contrary is proved the minutes establish that the meetings were duly convened and held and that the proceedings were conducted as the minutes record. But unless the articles so provide the minutes are not conclusive evidence, i.e. other evidence of what occurred may be produced. *Table A Article 58* provides an example of minutes as conclusive evidence as it provides that a declaration by the chairman that a resolution has been carried on a show of hands shall (unless a poll is then demanded) be conclusive if it is duly minuted that the resolution was so carried.

(c) Minutes books of general meetings must be kept at the registered office and must be open for inspection by members for at least two hours on business days free of charge. A member may also demand a copy of the minutes at a charge not exceeding 10p per 100 words: *s. 52 CA 1967*. There are no such rights in respect of minutes of directors' meetings.

ANSWER D29

If Wye Holdings Ltd wish to simplify the capital structure of the group for their own administrative convenience they must offer the holders of the preference shares sufficiently attractive alternatives to be a real inducement. The holding company would presumably only want a total reconstruction with no outstanding anomalies.

Wye could therefore offer the preference shareholders cash or other shares, or a combination as consideration for their shares.

One type of offer that has become popular is an exchange of shares, e.g. shares in Wye for the preference shares in the various companies with a 'cash alternative', i.e. the right for a limited period to sell the Wye shares received in exchange to a purchaser (generally found by the holding company) for cash.

A straightforward sale of preference shares to Wye would solve their problems if Wye can achieve 100% acceptance, but it can be expected that a minority of shareholders in the subsidiaries will either ignore or reject any offer made to them. Wye may still realise its wishes by promoting either a scheme of arrangement under *s. 206 CA 1948* or *s. 287 CA 1948* or by compulsory acquisition under *s. 209 CA 1948*.

Under *s. 206* a company may suggest any form of compromise, arrangement etc., but the terms of acquisition must be set out in a scheme document (supported by an explanatory note). A summons must then be made to the court asking it to order the calling of the necessary meetings to approve the scheme. Each company involved in the scheme must then convene the meetings and obtain a majority vote representing three quarters in value of the class approving the scheme. It is essential that separate meetings should be held of every group of shareholders whose interests as a group are differently affected, e.g. by national tax systems; it may even be necessary to subdivide the members of a particular class of shareholders: *Re Hellenic & General Trust Ltd* (*1976*). Once the meetings have sanctioned the scheme the court is petitioned for its approval.

The court must be satisfied that the statutory provisions have been compiled with, e.g. if the scheme includes a reduction of capital or variation of class rights the appropriate measures must have been taken, and that the various classes and minorities have been fairly represented. The scheme takes effect immediately on the court's order and is binding on all parties: *s. 208 CA 1948*.

S. 287 gives power to a company to reconstruct by means of a voluntary liquidation wherein the liquidator transfers the assets of the company to a new company in exchange for shares or securities of the new company. If Wye could obtain the required special resolution for putting the various companies into voluntary liquidation and then exchange the shares in those companies for shares in Wye this would effect a simple amalgamation without the requirement of court sanction. *S. 287* procedure does have the disadvantage that any member who did not vote on the resolution for voluntary liquidation may leave a note of his dissent with the company requiring the liquidator to refrain from the scheme. If the liquidator wishes to continue he must purchase the interest of the dissenting member.

An alternative procedure is to make separate offers for the outstanding shares of each company. If acceptances are received within four months from shareholders who hold not less than 90% of the shares for which each offer is separately made, Wye may within two months give notice to the non-accepting shareholders (treating each company minority separately) of its intention to compulsorily acquire their shares on the same terms (including any 'cash alternative': *Re Carlton Holdings* (*1971*). The shareholders may within one month apply to the court to order that their shares shall not be so acquired, otherwise the acquisition proceeds.

The main advantages of a scheme under *s. 206* is that it requires approval by only a three-quarters majority of votes cast at the meeting, whereas compulsory acquisition under *s. 209* requires 90% acceptance first. A scheme, however, entails the expense of two court hearings but it can be so designed to avoid payment of stamp duty by cancelling the outstanding shares instead of acquiring them.

Finally, Wye through its control of the ordinary shares of the various companies can solve its administrative problems by a reduction of capital to pay off the preference shareholders under *s. 66 CA 1948* but this is a rather cumbersome method. This would entail every company having the power in its articles to reduce or giving itself the power by altering the articles (*s. 10 CA 1948*) by special resolution and passing a special resolution of the company exercising the power to reduce. If it is not proposed to treat shareholders in accordance with their rights the normal practice is first to vary them by separate class meetings under a variation clause. Finally, it would be necessary to apply to the court for confirmation of the reduction.

ANSWER D30

(a) A liquidator appointed in a voluntary winding up must within 14 days of appointment give notice of it to the Registrar and publish it in the *London Gazette: s. 305 CA 1948*.

(b) It is assumed that the articles (as in *Article 76* of *Table A*) provide that the directors' remuneration shall be voted in general meeting. If that is so they were not competent to vote remuneration to themselves and may be required to refund it: *Re Whitehall Court* (*1887*). If, however, the directors were also the only shareholders it is possible that they may be held to have approved the payments in their capacity of shareholders: *Re Duomatic Ltd* (*1969*) (the 'assent principle').

(c) It is assumed that in creating the charge the directors acted in good faith and that the charge was duly registered: *s. 95 CA 1948*. It may nonetheless be set aside as a floating charge created within 12 months of winding up unless it can be shown that the company was solvent, i.e. able to pay its debts, at the time: *McClay v McQueen* (*1899*); *s. 322 CA 1948*. If this condition cannot be met the charge is invalid except to the extent that it secured loans paid in cash to the company (with interest at 5% per annum) at the time of and in consideration of the charge. If, as the question implies, it was given to secure an existing obligation it would be invalid.

The charge might also be void as a fraudulent preference since it was created six months before winding up commenced: *s. 320 CA 1948*. In this case it must be shown that at a time when the company was unable to pay its debts as they fell due it was created voluntarily with the dominant intention of preferring one creditor to others: *Re Kushler Ltd* (*1943*). It would not however be voluntary if it was given to a creditor who was threatening legal proceedings unless given security.

ANSWER D31

If a company in liquidation is insolvent, *s. 317 CA 1948* states that the same rules concerning priority of debts are to apply as in the case of bankruptcies (as far as the provisions of the *Bankruptcy Act 1914* are applicable to companies). This means that the costs of the liquidation will be paid first. Second in the order of priority will be preferential debts as defined in *s. 319* as amended, and third will come the ordinary creditors. (The question does not indicate the existence of any fixed or floating charge.)

The liquidator in the situation described in the question therefore needs to decide which debts are preferential and which are ordinary. On the surface Money Bank appears to be an unsecured ordinary creditor. However, where the money advanced for the purpose is paid to a clerk, servant, workman or labourer in respect of wages, salary or holiday pay, the lender of the money is entitled to the same priority as would have been enjoyed by that employee. One of the preferential debts according to *s. 319* as amended is the wages or salary of any clerk or servant in respect of services rendered during the four months immediately prior to the 'relevant date'. The relevant date in the case of a company in voluntary liquidation is the date of the winding up resolution. There is however an upper limit of £800 per employee. Assuming that the company's six employees are in fact employees and not labour-only sub-contractors, £4,800 of the £6,000 advanced by

Money Bank will be a preferential debt. This is an application of the doctrine of subrogation under which the lender stands in the place of the employees and claims in their right. The bank will rank as an ordinary creditor for the remaining £1,200.

Income Tax deducted under PAYE from employees' remuneration within the twelve months immediately before the relevant date is also a preferential debt. The liquidator will have to apportion £4,000 claimed by the Inland Revenue accordingly. Clearly some of it will be a preferential debt and for the balance the Inland Revenue will rank as an ordinary creditor.

The liquidator may seek to swell the company's assets by making a claim against Jones based on the misfeasance by Jones in taking for himself discount which he obtained on the goods purchased on the company's behalf. In this respect, Jones has made a secret profit in breach of his fiduciary duties as a director of the company.

Here, a misfeasance summons under *s. 333* will be appropriate. Jones as a director is an officer of the company within the meaning of *s. 455* and therefore the court has power to order that any such person should pay or restore all money or property which he has misapplied or retained or for which he has become liable or accountable or to contribute such sums to the assets of the company by way of compensation as the court thinks fit. The liquidator should make an appropriate application, subject to not wishing to waste costs by doing so if Jones if penniless.

The question mentions that Jones committed the company to several risky speculative transactions. The liquidator should consider whether this amounted to fraudulent trading under *s. 332*. The court may impose personal liability for all or any part of the company's debts or other liabilities upon any persons who were knowingly parties to fraudulent trading. Did Jones carry on the company's business with intent to defraud creditors or for fraudulent purpose? The result will depend on what evidence is available to the liquidator, but on the basis of *Re William C Leitch Bros Ltd* (*1932*) there will be an inference of fraudulent trading if Jones knew there was no reasonable prospect of the creditors ever receiving payment of the debts he was incurring. It seems, however, that it will be necessary to adduce some evidence of actual hishonesty: *Re Patrick & Lyon Ltd* (*1933*). If fraudulent trading cannot be proved, it may be possible for the liquidator to claim damages from Jones on the basis of common law negligence (i.e. the breach of his duties of skill and care in managing the company's affairs).

The liquidator may also seek repayment from the bank of the amount paid to it by the company to eliminate the ovedraft and to secure the release of Jones's guarantee. The facts are similar to those in *Re Kuchler Ltd* (*1943*) in which Kushler and his wife were directors of a company whose overdraft they had guaranteed and they ensured that in order to obtain a release of their guarantee the bank was repaid with company funds while the trade creditors were paid nothing. The basis of the decision was what is now *s. 320* relating to 'fraudulent' or 'voidable' preferences. The section applies to transactions in the course of which the company parts with money or property within the six months prior to the commencement of the liquidation and at a time when it was insolvent.

For the section to apply there must be a dominant intention to prefer one creditor over the others. In a case like *Re Kushler* there is no evidence of intention but the circumstances speak for themselves and a dominant intention to prefer the bank is inferred. It would be otherwise in the case of payments in the ordinary course of trade or where there is clearly no voluntary decision to prefer but the payment is made in response to threats.

If in this case the liquidator is able to obtain repayment from the bank on the basis of *s. 320*, the bank will in turn be able to recover the money from Jones, assuming he is able to pay. The court dealing with the fraudulent preference claim has power to adjudicate on the position between the bank and Jones as guarantor and to restore to the bank its rights under the released guarantee.

ANSWER D32

Circumstances frequently arise in which a company may find it expedient to reconstruct its undertaking or to amalgamate with another company or enter into some arrangement or compromise with its members or creditors or some particular class or classes of members or creditors. The terms 'reconstruction' and 'amalgamation' are loosely used commercial expressions not defined in the Companies Acts.

(a) A reconstruction may be purely internal or may be external. An internal reconstruction often involves a re-organisation of the company's capital usually to simplify and rationalise an unduly complicated capital structure such as is often found in older companies with many different classes of shares. The members will be invited to consent to variation of their rights to achieve this and often an application to the court will be necessary for approval of a reduction of capital (*ss. 66–69 CA 1948*). The necessary changes to the memorandum and articles of association will need to be made.

An external reconstruction involves the transfer by the company of its undertaking and assets to a new company (usually formed for the purpose) in exchange for shares in the new company. These shares are then distributed to the shareholders in the old company. In this way the new company has acquired and carries on substantially the same business as the old company with substantially the same shareholders. This may be achieved by using, *s. 287 CA 1948*, in which the old company goes into voluntary liquidation, the liquidator effects the transaction and the old company is then dissolved. Such a reconstruction may be useful in a variety of circumstances, e.g. to hive off part of an existing company's business or split its business between two or more new companies.

(b) An amalgamation, otherwise called a merger, may be achieved by means of a reconstruction as in (a) above, or by the acquiring company (new or already in existence) allotting shares to the members of the old company (the 'target' company being acquired) in exchange for their shares in that company: such an acquisition in exchange for shares, or a mixture of shares, debentures or cash, is usually intended to give rise to a holding/subsidiary company relationship. Thus, a merger may be effected by either acquisition of assets (the business is bought) or an acquisition of shares (the company is bought).

(c) Any form of reconstruction or amalgamation usually involves members or creditors or both in giving up rights in exchange for some other benefit. This is a compromise or arrangement. A minority might not be prepared to accept the terms and there is therefore machinery under *s. 206 CA 1948* for obtaining court approval of such a scheme. The court will examine the fairness of the scheme but if there is a favourable 75% majority of the members or creditors who attend and vote at separate meetings called for that purpose, the court usually sanctions the scheme and it then binds the dissenting minority. *S. 206* is useful in any compromise with members or creditors but if in a proposed amalgamation there is no co-operation by the board of the 'target' company, it cannot be used. The 'take-over' procedure specified in *s. 209* may then come into play: offers will be made direct to the shareholders in the target company for the purchase of their shares and (subject to the detailed provisions of the section) if 90% in value accept, the bidding company may compulsorily acquire the shares of the non-accepting minority.